DINNER CHEZ MOI

Also by **ELIZABETH BARD**

Picnic in Provence

Lunch in Paris

DINNER CHEZ MOI

50 French Secrets to Joyful Eating and Entertaining

ELIZABETH BARD

Little, Brown and Company

NEW YORK • BOSTON • LONDON

Little, Brown and Company
Hachette Book Group
1290 Avenue of the Americas, New York, NY 10104
littlebrown.com

First Edition: April 2017

Little, Brown and Company is a division of Hachette Book Group, Inc. The Little, Brown name and logo are trademarks of Hachette Book Group, Inc.

The publisher is not responsible for websites (or their content) that are not owned by the publisher.

The Hachette Speakers Bureau provides a wide range of authors for speaking events. To find out more, go to hachettespeakersbureau.com or call (866) 376-6591.

Illustrations by Virginia Johnson

ISBN 978-0-316-27625-2
LCCN 2016954209

10 9 8 7 6 5 4 3 2 1

LSC-C

Book design by Fearn Cutler de Vicq

Printed in the United States of America

For Rachel

CONTENTS

viii

Contents

DINNER CHEZ MOI

WHERE I BEGAN

onjour! Before we begin, a word—and it's an important one: I'm an American. Though I've lived in France for fifteen years and now hold two passports, I grew up in Bruce Springsteen's U.S.A. of the 1980s, eating instant macaroni and cheese, General Tso's chicken, and Pillsbury vanilla frosting out of the can. I did not have a French grandmother who made me leek soup or served me fish with the head on. Like almost everyone I knew, I ate baked beans and fish sticks. Cheese meant fluorescent orange Kraft singles. I did not know anything about the pleasures of champagne cocktails or the digestive benefits of herbal teas. The radical change in my eating habits came when I moved to France, at the age of twenty-eight, to be with my French husband, Gwendal. I discovered a culture of fresh seasonal ingredients, the pleasure of cooking for and eating with family and friends, and ingredients I'd never thought about, like lentils and almond flour, that have become staples of a heartier—and healthier—diet. I'm not a chef; I'm a home cook who was delighted to discover that good things don't take all day to prepare, and that if you start with great ingredients, a great dinner is almost inevitable. I'm writing this book because I know it is possible to change ingrained eating habits, even in adulthood, and because I know these are changes a lot of people are trying to make—in ways big and small—in their own kitchens. I hope this book is equal parts inspiring, helpful, and fun!

Part One

INGREDIENTS

I will never forget my first trips to the Tuesday-morning market on the rue de Belleville in Paris. The fishmonger asked me for a date over glassy-eyed whole mackerel, and the man who sold me green beans called me his *gazelle*. I bought myself a bouquet of fresh herbs instead of flowers and tasted a plump fresh fig for the first time—an almost religious experience. For the first few weeks I stayed away from the hairy beige bowling ball that turned out to be a very tasty celery root. There was definitely some impatient foot-tapping behind me at the local butcher as I slowly mastered the vocabulary necessary to order my *épaule d'agneau désossée,* deboned shoulder of lamb.

Unless you're a born cook, or a bit of a mad scientist, most of us have a fear of new ingredients. We cook what we know. This chapter breaks down the essentials of my French kitchen; some of them will be familiar, some more mysterious. I've divided my list into pantry staples, a few things I always have in my fridge, and some new things you should try the next time you see them (in season!) at the market. I've provided an easy-to-follow recipe for each to help you along in your culinary discoveries and, where appropriate, some ways to dress things up for guests. Where relevant I've also recommended brands that will get you as close as possible to the authentic French taste.

MY FRENCH PANTRY

I'm a cook who likes a full pantry. I love to go hunting through my cabinets on a rainy day and see what I can create without a trip to the store. Here are some of the things I always have in stock:

Secret #1

A decent bottle of olive oil: Not a single day goes by that I don't reach for my bottle of olive oil—for salad dressing, roasting vegetables, making pasta sauce, browning meat, even baking. A tablespoon of olive oil is the single best way I've found to get friendly with green vegetables—it elevates them from merely virtuous to outright delicious. I know good olive oil can be expensive in the States. In Provence, we are spoiled; it's basically the same price as bottled water. Although olive oil tends to be associated with Italy, the Spanish section of your local supermarket is also a good place to look.

Tip

I buy my olive oil in three-liter jugs

from my local butcher (it's cheaper that way) and

decant into a smaller bottle. I recommend having one bottle

of fruity extra-virgin olive oil for sauces and salad dressing

and one bottle of milder ordinary olive oil

for everyday cooking and baking.

HARICOTS VERTS IN OLIVE OIL

Haricots verts à l'huile d'olive

Many of our weekday meals include a single serving of protein and a big heap of seasonal vegetables (green beans, leeks, brussels sprouts, Swiss chard, or spinach) cooked with olive oil. My method is somewhere between steam and sauté—I find this keeps the fresh taste and gives you the delicious charred bits everyone loves. In my humble opinion, slim French haricots verts beat the pants off regular old green beans and are worth searching around for. They cook quickly yet retain their signature snap. If you decide to use thicker, American-style green beans, you may want to blanch them in boiling water for thirty seconds (then run them under cold water to stop the cooking) and proceed with your recipe from there.

1½ pounds haricots verts (extra-slim French green beans), topped but not tailed

2 to 3 tablespoons extra-virgin olive oil

Coarse sea salt

Freshly ground black pepper

Serves 4 as a side dish; if doubling, make two batches (the beans won't char if they are crowded)

Rinse trimmed green beans in a colander—no need to dry them. In fact, you want some water clinging to them; it will help them steam.

In a large frying or sauté pan with a lid, heat oil. Add green beans and stir to coat. Cover and cook over medium-high heat for 3 minutes. Stir and add a good sprinkle of sea salt.

Cover and cook for 4 to 6 more minutes, stirring every 3 minutes or so. Don't worry if you see some charred bits—that's my favorite part. Taste and see if the beans are cooked through. If not, give them another 3 minutes. Transfer to a serving platter. Add a pinch or two of salt to taste and a good grinding of black pepper.

Serve warm or at room temperature. If you have leftovers (doubtful), eat them topped with big chunks of tuna or a poached egg for lunch the next day.

Dress Up: If you want a gussied-up version of this dish for guests, replace one tablespoon of the olive oil with walnut oil and top with some toasted walnuts before serving.

Try this

Substitute olive oil for all or part of the vegetable oil

in your favorite banana bread (or zucchini bread, or carrot cake—

you get the idea). I use olive oil to make my French yogurt cake

(see page 63). I recently started using olive oil

to make my stovetop popcorn!

**Secret
#2**

Coarse sea salt: Salt is a culinary enlivener—it makes other ingredients taste just a bit more like themselves. But salt requires control, something I've never achieved with a grinder or shaker. I keep my salt in a covered container handy to the stove, so I can take a pinch whenever I need it. If coarse sea salt seems an unnecessary extravagance, think again. The French would tell you that little things make a big difference. And why buy something that is more refined than necessary? Highly processed table salts with iodine and anticaking agents fulfill a function but have no taste. Sea-salt crystals have a very specific *terroir*, as individual as the mineral content of the body of water they come from. They are also beautiful—like topping your food with a scattering of tiny diamonds. *Attention!* You will notice that almost all the recipes in this book (even the baked goods) specify coarse sea salt. You can use kosher salt in a pinch, but please DO NOT substitute the same amount of regular table salt (or fine sea salt). Because of the fine grain, one teaspoon of table salt actually contains more salt than a whole tablespoon of coarse sea salt!

✎ Accessories ✑

When I used to give tours at the Louvre Museum, I would stop to admire an ornate gold-and-agate saltcellar that once belonged to Louis XIV. (The French have always taken their tableware *very* seriously.) A saltcellar is a small bowl of sea salt that the French often put on the table instead of a shaker. When I got married, my friend Amanda's mom sent me a crystal saltcellar complete with miniature wooden spoon. This may seem old-fashioned, but hey, I'm an old-fashioned girl, so of course I loved it. It also turned out to be one of my most useful gifts. I use salt sparingly in my French cooking; if my guests want to add salt, the tiny spoon lets them see exactly how many grains they are adding to their plates. Next time you are looking for a hostess gift for a foodie friend, why not arrive with a small jar of exotic sea salt and a wooden saltcellar!

Secret #3

A bottle of sherry vinegar or red wine vinegar: I considered calling this book *French Women Don't Buy Salad Dressing.* The way the French make salad dressing says a lot about their culinary philosophy in general: fine ingredients, simply combined.

All you really need to make perfect salad dressing are your first three pantry ingredients: olive oil, sea salt, and vinegar. Most French people I know mix them right in the bottom of the salad bowl and gently toss the leaves on top. This method has lots of advantages. When you mix from the bottom, you rarely drown your greens. Just toss until the salad is very lightly coated; any extra will remain at the bottom, so you might get one soggy leaf but not a whole soggy bowl. You can add a dab of Dijon or whole-grain mustard and a clove of crushed garlic if you like, but stay away from honey and other sweet ingredients—the French don't want to eat dessert on their salad.

I prefer sherry vinegar to plain red wine vinegar; it's just a bit more robust. I do have balsamic vinegar in my cabinet, but I find it too sweet and heavy for traditional French vinaigrette; I keep it around for tomatoes with mozzarella in the summer. In addition to dressing salads, vinegar will help you make a great pan sauce with fruit (duck with blackberries, anyone?), give zing to grilled sardines, and add a sweet-sour kick to honey-braised cabbage.

MY FAVORITE FRENCH VINAIGRETTE

Vinaigrette à l'ail

When I arrived in France, I was floored by the number of different kinds of lettuce—delicate *mâche*, frilly violet Batavia, spiny bitter frisée.

French vinaigrette is like your favorite lip gloss; it should add the merest shimmer of flavor. Above all, you want the taste and texture of the salad leaves to shine through. This is the way Gwendal's grandparents made vinaigrette. Don't be scared of a little raw garlic—the French certainly aren't—but don't overdo it either. I've given quantities here for one average-size head of lettuce to be mixed directly in the bottom of the salad bowl.

2 tablespoons extra-virgin olive oil

1½ teaspoons sherry vinegar (in the summer, I often use fresh-squeezed lemon juice)

2 generous pinches of coarse sea salt

A good grind of black pepper

½ teaspoon whole-grain or Dijon mustard

1 small clove garlic, finely grated or pushed through a press

Pinch of herbes de Provence, ñora pepper, or smoked paprika (optional)

Dresses 1 average-size head of lettuce

Whisk all the ingredients together directly in the bottom of your salad bowl. Just before serving, add lettuce leaves and toss until lightly coated.

Trick: You might measure at first, but you'll soon be eyeing it like a pro. I think of vinaigrette in terms of concentric circles: If the disk of olive oil in the bottom of my bowl is the diameter of a softball, I want my disk of vinegar to be about the diameter of a quarter. Add a pinch of salt, whisk, taste, and see how you feel.

Attention!

If you are opening the 1953 Château Margaux

your parents have been saving for a special occasion,

the French would tell you to dress your salad with

only olive oil and a little salt. Vinegar will

alter the taste of the wine.

"Pardon me. Would you have any Grey Poupon?"
the ad used to say. Why, yes, I certainly do. Dijon
mustard is the only condiment you will see regularly on
a French bistro table. Ketchup is for tourists. Dab Dijon
on steak and sausage, add it sparingly to your now-
perfect French vinaigrette, or mix a little with crème
fraîche for braised leeks. My mother-in-law taught me
to smear a little on the bottom of the tart crust when
making a quiche.

I won't pretend this is a recipe, but if you want a
wonderful side dish for chicken: Cut 3 leeks (white
and light green parts only) into ½-inch rounds. Boil
for 1 minute; drain. Heat 1 tablespoon olive oil in a
large saucepan. Add the leeks, a sprinkle of salt, and a
good grind of black pepper and sauté for 10 minutes,
stirring occasionally. Just before serving, add a
teaspoon of Dijon mustard and a tablespoon of crème
fraîche or sour cream. Yum.

Secret #4

Wine: With the amount of wine in my cooking, I should be drunk off the fumes. I'm a cheap date; I probably use more wine in my recipes every week than I drink in a month. Red, white, rosé—wine is plentiful and cheap in France, so it shows up at pretty much every meal. It is my base liquid for stews and braises, makes wonderful syrup for poached pears, and completes a quick pasta sauce with garlic and tomatoes. In the summertime, there always seems to be a bottle open from some early-evening *apéro* (wine that's a few days old and a bit off for drinking is fine for cooking). In the winter I often buy cheap boxes of white and red wine, the kind with the spigot that lasts for weeks. Handy for poaching plums, making pot roast, and oven-roasting fish.

Tip: I use a dribble of white wine instead of water to add flavor and moisture when defrosting soup or lentils.

OVEN-ROASTED MONKFISH WITH WHITE WINE, CURED HAM, AND GREEN OLIVES

Papillotes de lotte au jambon cru

These little fish parcels wrapped in cured ham are elegant enough for a dinner party but easy enough to make on a weeknight. If you can't find monkfish, thick cod fillets are a good substitute. The salty crisp of the ham provides a nice contrast to the meaty white fish, and the wine keeps everything moist in the oven. One Christmas, my mother-in-law and I made this with whole sea bass. She added plump green olives to the mix—the result was so good, I've been doing it that way ever since.

3 tablespoons olive oil

6 monkfish fillets, 5 ounces each

Coarse sea salt

Freshly ground black pepper

1 tomato, cut into 6 thin slices

6 thin slices of cured ham, such as prosciutto

12 green olives, such as picholine or manzanilla

½ cup dry white wine

¼ teaspoon fresh or dried thyme leaves or a pinch of herbes de Provence

Serves 6

Preheat the oven to 375°F. Put the olive oil in a 9-by-13-inch casserole dish. Roll the fish fillets in the olive oil and sprinkle with a little coarse sea salt and a grind of black pepper. Roll the tomato slices around in the oil as well, then top each fillet with a tomato and wrap the fish with a slice of cured ham. Add the olives and white wine, then sprinkle with fresh or dried thyme. Cook for 30 to 35 minutes, depending on the thickness of the fillets. This is excellent (and very pretty!) served on a bed of wilted spinach with a side of sweet potato puree. If I wanted to make a paleo dinner party without anyone noticing, this would be the main course.

Secret
#5

Chickpeas: Cheap, nutritious, and available year-round, chickpeas are the backup singers of my Provençal cooking. I always keep three or four cans in the pantry; they are my go-to ingredient when I want to add heft to a lunchtime salad or need a quick side dish for whatever's on the grill (see Whole-Grain Salad with Chickpeas and Herbs, page 58). Though we tend to associate them with the other side of the Mediterranean, chickpeas have made their mark on Provençal cuisine. They pop up everywhere, from *socca*, the traditional chickpea-flour crepes made in Nice, to *poichichade,* the garlicky Provençal equivalent of hummus. Now that we live in a tiny village of thirteen hundred people, there's not a ton of choice when I crave more exotic tastes (i.e., takeout), so I use chickpeas to make a simple vegetarian curry (Google Nigella Lawson's chickpea curry) or for my improvised garlic ginger shrimp.

SPICED CHICKPEAS
WITH GARLIC GINGER SHRIMP

Crevettes et pois chiches aux épices

This is what I make on a weeknight when I rush in the door and feel like I have to start cooking with my coat on. With a can of chickpeas, a few herbs and spices, and a bag of shrimp from the freezer, I can make one of my family's favorite dinners in ten minutes.

1 28-ounce can chickpeas, drained and rinsed

3 tablespoons olive oil (you can use part sesame oil if you have it on hand)

1-inch piece of fresh ginger, finely grated

4 large cloves garlic, finely grated

½ teaspoon garam masala (or use half cumin, half pumpkin-pie spice plus a pinch of paprika and/or hot pepper)

Coarse sea salt and black pepper

1-pound bag of frozen *raw* shrimp (they will be gray, rather than pink, in the bag)

1 handful fresh cilantro, finely chopped

½ lemon

Serves 2 adults and 1 little guy (i.e., my family) for a light dinner

In a colander, rinse and drain the chickpeas. I like to rub off and discard the waxy skins, but it's not strictly necessary. In a large sauté pan, heat the olive oil over medium-high heat. Add the ginger and garlic and sauté for 30 seconds. Add the chickpeas, spices, and a good sprinkle of salt and pepper. Sauté for 3 to 4 minutes, scraping the bottom of the pan so the garlic and ginger don't burn. When the chickpeas start to make a sound like popcorn, lower the heat, remove the chickpeas from the pot, and place them on a serving platter. Put the heat back up to medium-high and add the frozen shrimp. Use the water they give off to scrape the garlicky ginger goodness from the bottom of the pan. Cover and cook until the shrimp are pink and just cooked through (this won't take long). Add the shrimp to the serving platter and top with a handful of cilantro and a good squeeze of lemon.

Secret #6

Lentils: A big pot of lentils with sausage is my definition of French comfort food. I don't know why I never cooked with lentils in the States; it might be because somewhere in my mind they were linked with the sludgy brown mass of 1970s vegetarian meat loaf. Lentils are standard family fare in France, used in winter stews and cold summer salads. They also freeze well, so I always make a big batch and put half in the freezer for another meal.

Try this

From Middle Eastern **mujaddara** to Peruvian **tacu tacu** and Indian **khichdi,** rice and lentils are natural partners. If you are looking to add protein to any rice dish, boil ½ cup of lentils for 15 minutes, drain, and stir into the raw rice before cooking.

LENTIL AND SAUSAGE STEW

Lentilles aux saucisses fumées

This is a favorite dish in our house year-round—warm and comforting as a big bear hug. Friends and family request it each time they visit, even if it's 100 degrees in the shade!

2 tablespoons olive oil

2 pounds high-quality smoked sausage, such as Jésu de Morteau, sliced into 2-inch rounds (or use Toulouse or Italian sausages, left whole)

2 medium carrots, finely chopped

2 medium onions, diced

1 small bulb fennel, finely chopped

2 stalks celery with leaves, chopped

1 large handful flat-leaf parsley, chopped (use some stems as well), plus more for serving

2 cloves garlic, peeled but left whole

2 pounds Le Puy lentils

3 sun-dried tomatoes, chopped

1 cup white wine

1 bay leaf

Freshly ground black pepper

12 cups very hot or boiling water

Dijon mustard, for serving

Serves 6 to 8

Ingredients

In a large Dutch oven or stockpot, heat the olive oil and brown the sausages. Add the vegetables, parsley, and garlic, stir to coat, and sauté until softened, about 10 minutes. Add lentils and sun-dried tomatoes; stir to coat. Add wine; it will sizzle a bit. Add bay leaf and a good grinding of black pepper. Add the very hot or boiling water. Bring to a boil, turn down heat, and simmer, cover slightly ajar, until lentils are tender and most of the liquid is absorbed—50 minutes to 1 hour. I don't add salt to this dish, as the sausage tends to take care of that. I used to add a bouillon cube to the water at the beginning, but now I prefer the purer taste of the lentils and veggies.

Serve a hefty bowl of lentils with the sausage on top. Accompany with Dijon mustard and more chopped parsley.

Tip: I nearly always get two meals out of this. It freezes well; reheat with a few tablespoons of white wine. If you still have leftover lentils after all the sausage is gone, serve them with broiled salmon fillets or puree with 1 part white wine and 2 parts chicken broth to make a thick soup. Serve the soup (or the salmon, for that matter) with a squeeze of lime, a dollop of crème fraîche or Greek yogurt, and lots of chopped cilantro.

๛ Fun Fact ๑
Two American staples
you'll never find in a French kitchen

Peanut butter: Do not make peanut butter cookies when a French family moves in next door. The French have only experienced peanut butter in Asian or African cuisine, as part of the savory sauce for mafé, for example. They just don't get the sweet version.

Corn: Most people in France think corn is something you feed to animals. You can find popcorn at the movies (*not* to be eaten during a serious film), but it's not an ingredient French people tend to cook with. Every time I convert a French person to my corn soufflé at Thanksgiving, I feel a little burst of American triumph.

Farro: *Petit épeautre* (einkorn wheat) is an ingredient that I discovered when we moved to Provence. In the States, it is easier to find one of its cousins, emmer wheat, often sold under the Italian name *farro*.

There's been a lot of whole-grain hoopla in the States over the past few years, but the French eat farro for the same reason they eat everything else—because it tastes good. An ancient form of wheat, the grains function a lot like barley, perfect for a thick winter soup, a cold salad with lots of herbs and veggies, or a whole-grain risotto with a bite. I love the nutty taste and firm texture. Serve farro instead of rice with stuffed cabbage, pot roast, or any dish with lots of sauce to soak up. Farro is terrific if you want a risotto-like texture without the constant supervision.

Try this

Cook one pound of farro according to the manufacturer's
directions. Drain and freeze in one-cup portions. Add to your
favorite chicken noodle soup, clam chowder, or minestrone.
Farro's satisfying texture and whole-grain goodness
can turn a cup-a-soup into a full meal!

Nobody wants to speak Latin at the supermarket, but buying farro can be confusing; vague labeling means you may have to read the fine print to find out exactly what you're getting.

farro piccolo; in French, **petit épeautre** (einkorn);
>   **Triticum monococcum**

farro medio (emmer); **Triticum dicoccum**

farro grande (spelt); **Triticum spelta**

Emmer and einkorn can cook up firm and nutty for salads but will burst into a creamy risotto texture if you cook them long enough. Spelt is like that girl in high school, impervious—best for salads, when you don't want anything to get mushy. Pearled and semi-pearled varieties will cook up faster for everyday use. Whole grains (hulled) hold up better in soups and stews. **Petit épeautre (einkorn) is the only form of wheat that has never been hybridized, and so, although it's not gluten-free, it is more easily digested by some people with gluten intolerance.** If you are new to all this, I would suggest Bob's Red Mill brand for farro (emmer) and spelt, and the Jovial brand for einkorn.

PROVENÇAL FARRO RISOTTO

Risotto de petit épeautre à la Provençal

This recipe is somewhere between a soup, a stew, and a risotto—in other words, all my favorite things. It would be hard to fit more good—and good for you—things into a single pot. This is an excellent alternative to vegetarian chili when you are cooking for a crowd. Serve with a handful of grated Gruyère for an extra-creamy feel.

3 tablespoons olive oil

1 red onion, chopped

1 small bulb fennel, including fronds, chopped

3 carrots, chopped

1 large stalk celery with leaves, chopped

1 trimmed leek (white and light green parts), finely chopped

2 cloves garlic, chopped

3 tablespoons tomato paste

Freshly ground black pepper

1 pound farro or einkorn wheat berries—not the quick-cooking (pearled) kind!

2 small zucchini, chopped

1 cup dry white wine

1 14-ounce can crushed tomatoes (or 1 pound fresh tomatoes, peeled and chopped)

11 cups low-sodium chicken or
    vegetable broth (as there is
    no canned broth in France, I use
    water with 2 bouillon cubes)
1 28-ounce can red kidney beans,
    drained and rinsed
A few sprigs fresh thyme
    (or 2 pinches dried thyme)
Grated Gruyère (to serve)

Serves 8

In a large stockpot, heat the olive oil. Sauté the onion, fennel, carrots, celery, and leek until softened, about 8 minutes. Add garlic and cook for an additional 2 minutes. Add the tomato paste and a grind of black pepper. Stir for 1 minute. Add the farro and zucchini; stir to combine. Add the wine and tomatoes; stir to combine.

Add broth, beans, and thyme. Bring to a boil. Then turn down the heat and simmer over low heat for 45 minutes to 1 hour, mixing occasionally. You don't want to cook out all the liquid; the farro will continue to soak up the broth as it cools. Serve in shallow bowls with a handful of grated Gruyère. It freezes well; reheat with a small amount of broth or white wine.

**Secret
#8**

Split peas: I've never met a French person who didn't extol the virtues of soup. Whether it's a thick hearty peasant dish after a day of hiking, a quick vegetarian dinner, or a detoxifying broth for a Parisienne on her New Year's diet, soup is a staple of the French family table. It is most often made with fresh seasonal vegetables blended into a smooth velouté, but my fall/winter favorite is made with pork belly, split peas, and cognac. You can serve a small portion with a dollop of crème fraîche and some crumbled bacon as an appetizer or a larger bowl with bread, cheese, and salad for a full meal. My son calls this green soup *bave de dinosaure* (dinosaur spit), which, for him at least, makes it all the more appetizing.

SPLIT-PEA SOUP WITH PORK BELLY AND COGNAC

Soupe aux pois cassés

3 tablespoons olive oil

1 large carrot

1 large onion

1 small bulb fennel (including stalks and leaves)

1 small cinnamon stick (about 2 inches)

3 cloves (or a large pinch of ground cloves)

12-ounce piece of smoked pork belly or slab bacon

½ cup white wine

2 tablespoons cognac or brandy

2¼ pounds split green peas

1 bay leaf

1 chicken or vegetable bouillon cube (I use Knorr)

14 cups very hot or boiling water

Plain yogurt and freshly ground black pepper, for serving

Serves 8

In a large stockpot, heat the olive oil and sauté veggies, cinnamon, cloves, and pork belly or slab bacon until meat is browned and onion is translucent, about 10 to 12 minutes. (Stick the whole cloves into the surface of the meat; it keeps them from getting lost.)

Add white wine and let sizzle. Add cognac. Add split peas and stir. Add bay leaf. Dissolve bouillon cube in 1 cup boiling water. Add to the pot. Add remaining water. Bring to a boil. Lower heat and simmer with the cover slightly ajar, stirring occasionally, until the peas are tender, about 1½ hours.

Remove meat, bay leaf, cinnamon stick, and cloves. (If the cloves have gone missing, fish them out with a slotted spoon.) Blend soup with an immersion blender. Slice the meat and remove any fatty bits. Serve the soup with slices of pork belly on top, or with a dollop of plain yogurt and a grinding of black pepper.

There's no point in making a small batch of this soup—there will always be another blizzard, and it freezes perfectly. To reheat, dilute with a bit of white wine. I often sauté some extra bacon to crumble into the soup when I serve it the second time.

Note: You won't want to add any salt to the soup, as the pork belly or bacon and bouillon cube take care of that.

Secret #9

Cinnamon: "What's French about that?" you say. "I've been using cinnamon for years." Yes, but how? The French almost never use cinnamon in their baking. (My husband calls Starbucks Cinnamon Land because every pastry is so heavily laced with the stuff that you can't taste anything else.) Cinnamon is one of the principal spices of North African cuisine, where it is used in savory dishes as well as in desserts. Because of French colonial history, *la cuisine du Maghreb*—the cooking of Algeria, Morocco, and Tunisia—is the second cuisine of France; the French have adopted couscous and tagines the way Americans have adopted pizza and lasagna. Using cinnamon with meat and vegetables provides sweet and spicy undertones. Like wearing a red bra under your business suit, it changes everything, even though you might be the only one who knows it's there. Cinnamon looms large in my French kitchen for a very particular reason: My mother-in-law is what the French call a *pied noir*. Her grandparents moved from France to Morocco when the country was still a French protectorate. She was born in Casablanca, so we have many North African recipes in the family.

Tip: I always keep both whole cinnamon sticks and ground cinnamon on hand. I add cinnamon sticks to my tagines, mixed vegetable couscous, and split-pea soups, and a pinch of ground cinnamon adds warmth to oven-roasted vegetables, chickpea salad, and even tomato sauce.

NICOLE'S LAMB AND APRICOT TAGINE

Tajine d'agneau aux abricots

This is, hands down, one of my favorite meals. Fork-tender meat and sweet sauce–soaked apricots—your kitchen has never smelled so good. My mother-in-law keeps the spices simple, just cinnamon sticks and *piment doux* (a kind of sweet paprika), but I've added a tiny bit of fresh ginger for kicks. A traditional North African tagine would never include wine, but as this is my Frenchie version, I use half wine, half water. The best part about a tagine is that it really does taste better reheated, so it's a perfect make-ahead dish for company or a holiday dinner (I make lamb and prune tagine instead of my grandmother's tzimmes for Passover). Add a chickpea salad with cucumbers and feta to start, a big platter of fluffy couscous to soak up the sauce, and you have a perfect festive dinner for friends.

1 tablespoon olive oil

4 pounds lamb shoulder, cut into large chunks

Sea salt and freshly ground black pepper

4 medium onions

1 tablespoon paprika

2 cinnamon sticks (approximately 2 inches each)

3 "coins" of fresh ginger (each about ¼ inch thick and the size of a silver dollar)

2½ cups white wine

3 cups water

9 ounces whole dried apricots

3 ounces golden raisins

Toasted slivered almonds and fresh
    cilantro, to garnish (optional)

Serves 6

Preheat the oven to 350°F. In a large Dutch oven, heat olive oil and brown the meat in two batches. Sprinkle with sea salt and pepper along the way. Remove the meat and set aside in a separate bowl.

Add the onions and spices (paprika, cinnamon sticks, and ginger) to the hot oil. Over medium-low heat, stir to coat and wait until the onions wilt, about 7 to 10 minutes. Add ½ cup white wine; it will sizzle, and you'll be able to scrape any charred bits off the bottom of the pot. (It's important to start the sauce slowly and not add the liquid all at once.) Then add the remaining wine and the water and return the meat and its juices to the pot. Bring to a boil. Cover and transfer to the oven. Cook for 1 hour.

After the first hour, turn the meat, add the apricots and raisins, and stir. Make sure the apricots are submerged, so they soak up lots of sauce. Cover and return to the oven. Cook for an additional 1 to 1½ hours, until the meat is fork-tender and the sauce is beginning to reduce. Remove from the oven and let rest for a few hours or overnight. Though you can turn the meat once you take it out of the oven (again, to soak up the sauce), try not to disturb the fruit too much—you want the apricots to remain whole.

Reheat gently just before serving. Spoon the meat into a heated casserole dish and spoon the sauce and the dried fruit on top. You can garnish with toasted slivered almonds and fresh cilantro if you like.

Dress Up: If you want a more elegant look, make this tagine with lamb shanks—it will taste just as marvelous!

Secret #10

Herbal tea: And, *s'il vous plaît*, I don't mean Cozy Comfort Apple Cinnamon Pumpkin Pie Caramel Spice.

For centuries the French have ended their meals, helped their digestion, improved their circulation, and lessened their water retention with infusions—herbal teas made with actual plants and herbs. Drinking herbal tea after meals is now one of my most ingrained French habits (yet another thing I learned from my mother-in-law). In the evening, a mug of herbal tea and a square of dark chocolate tell my body that the kitchen is closed. One way to begin: Start with a single herb and see what you like. Try fresh or dried mint leaves in the afternoon (I now order mint tea at Starbucks), dried lemon verbena to aid digestion after a meal, and chamomile or orange flower just before bed. If you have a cold or sore throat, try infusing a few sprigs of fresh thyme in boiling water with a teaspoon of honey—it works wonders for respiratory infections. Herbal teas are 100 percent caffeine-free, so they are a great alternative if you are looking to cut down on coffee.

If you want to buy a blend, read the label carefully; aim for a straight list of herbs and spices. Many brands in the U.S. are bent on supporting our crippling love of sweets with "natural honey flavor" or "stevia extract." **A tisane is not supposed to be sweet—it's a daily cleansing ritual, not a substitute for dessert.** You may want to browse an upscale market or health-food store to avoid the wacko flavorings (I recently found an herbal tea called Sugar Cookie Sleigh Ride). Pure herbal teas might even be sold as "herbal supplements." Celestial Seasonings Sleepytime Classic is a good place to start—it's available in most supermarkets.

Slimming Secrets: **French women do not snack during the day**—they often drink tea between and after meals. It's an excellent way to stay hydrated and, as a result, to cut hunger.

**Secret
#11**

Dark chocolate: Meet your new best friend. This is French catnip; it's what the French reach for when they want *une gourmandise*—a little treat. Most of what is sold as dark chocolate in the U.S. is only 50 percent or 55 percent cacao. The French consider dark chocolate from 70 percent cacao upward (I'm addicted to the Lindt 85 percent). Check the cacao percentage in the list of ingredients. Even basic French supermarket baking chocolate, used for cakes and mousses, is 65 to 70 percent. You will spend more to buy high-quality chocolate, but I promise you'll taste the difference!

৵ Baking Chocolate ৵

The French cook with what we would call bittersweet chocolate, which has the sugar already added (as opposed to unsweetened chocolate, which doesn't). I can't imagine why, but the Lindt 70 percent baking chocolate that I buy for 1.48 euros at my local French supermarket costs a whopping twenty dollars a bar in the U.S.! If you want to bake French-style in the States, look for chocolate whose packaging states the exact cacao amount in it. The higher the percentage, the more bitter the chocolate. The equivalent to French chocolate is usually 60 to 72 percent cacao solids. If I moved back to the U.S. tomorrow, I would order a two-pound bag of Valrhona 72 percent or Callebaut 70 percent online. These come in the form of little coins, perfect for baking or judicious snacking. In a pinch, I might use Ghirardelli 60 percent baking bars, which are available in many supermarkets.

MY FAVORITE CHOCOLATE CAKE

Fondant au chocolat

When the French talk about chocolate cake, this is what they mean—a rich fudgy treat made with butter, the best-quality dark chocolate, and little, if any, flour. Along with a classic apple cake, most people have some version of this recipe in the family archives. *Fondant au chocolat* shows up at buffets and bake sales, but a small slice with a short espresso or glass of Armagnac is also a fine ending to a dinner party.

9 ounces dark chocolate (70 percent cacao)

14 tablespoons butter

6 eggs

1 cup sugar

1 scant cup almond meal

⅓ cup flour (use cornstarch or gluten-free flour to make this recipe gluten-free)

Serves 12

Preheat the oven to 350°F. Line the bottom of an 11-inch cake or springform pan with a disk of waxed paper. Melt the chocolate and butter together in the microwave or in the top of a double boiler; put aside to cool a bit. Separate the eggs into two large mixing bowls; put the whites in the fridge, and whisk the yolks with the sugar until a light lemon yellow. In a small bowl, stir together the almond meal and flour.

Add the warm chocolate mixture to the egg yolks and whisk quickly and thoroughly to combine. Add the flour mixture, and fold in with a spatula, just to combine. Beat the egg whites until they hold a stiff peak. Using a spatula or a wooden spoon, gently fold half the egg whites into the chocolate mixture, then fold in the rest.

Bake on the center rack for 15 minutes. Turn off the heat and let the cake rest 10 minutes in the oven with the door slightly ajar (I stick a wooden spoon in the door to hold it open). It will not look done when you take it out. Cool completely on a wire rack; the texture will set as it cools. I find this cake tastes even better the next day, so feel free to make it ahead of time. Serve at room temperature.

Secret #12

Almond flour (or meal): When friends started asking me about recipes for gluten-free desserts, I wasn't sure I had any in my repertoire. Then I realized, living in France, I've been making gluten-free sweets for years. Almond flour plays a big role in traditional French baking—it's in everything from the golden *financiers* sold at my favorite Paris boulangerie to the sweet frangipane base of my fig tart (see page 93).

Try this

Almond flour is not just for dessert.
Try substituting almond flour (toasted in a dry pan until golden) for bread crumbs in your meat loaf or veal Parmesan. I use a layer of toasted almond flour as a quick gluten-free crust for my leek and bacon quiche (page 84). We recently spent the weekend in Toulouse, where our friend Catherine made something superb. She roasted zucchini at 325°F for one hour, took it out, then added a crumble topping made from a mix of diced sun-dried tomatoes, olive oil (from the tomato jar), almond flour, and a little cornstarch. She put the whole thing back in the oven for twenty minutes, and voilà!

CLASSIC CHERRY CLAFOUTIS

Clafoutis aux cerises

Clafoutis is one of my favorite French comfort desserts. Somewhere between a custard and a cake, it is a showcase for seasonal fruit—most famously, the first cherries that arrive in June. Apricots, blackberries, or pears are also welcome. This is a great dish to bring to brunch or to end a casual dinner (I love it for breakfast straight from the fridge). I've been toying with my clafoutis recipe for years; one day I decided to add a cup of almond flour, and suddenly the texture was exactly what I wanted.

Butter and sugar (for tart mold)

2 whole eggs

2 egg yolks

¾ cup sugar

1 cup whipping cream
   (30 percent fat)

2 tablespoons rum, amaretto,
   or kirsch

¼ cup cornstarch

1 cup almond meal or flour

1⅛ cups milk

1 pound cherries, pitted

Serves 6 to 8

Preheat the oven to 400°F.

Butter and sugar a 10-inch ceramic tart mold.

In a large mixing bowl, whisk together the eggs, egg yolks, and sugar until they are a light lemon yellow. Gradually add the cream and the rum; whisk to combine. In a small bowl, combine cornstarch and almond meal. Add to the egg mixture; whisk thoroughly to combine. Slowly whisk in milk until thoroughly combined.

Add the pitted cherries to the bottom of the mold. Give the batter a final whisk and pour it around the cherries. Bake for 40 to 45 minutes, until well browned and set (but a bit wobbly) in the center. Serve warm or at room temperature.

Secret #13

Vanilla beans: I grew up baking with vanilla extract from the supermarket, which was mostly alcohol and artificial vanilla flavoring. The seeds of an actual vanilla bean, scraped into cake batter or infused into cream, will give your desserts the most marvelous aroma and taste. It's also a sensory trick—real vanilla suggests sweetness without adding extra sugar. Best of all, nothing goes to waste. Once you've scraped the seeds out of your vanilla bean, bury the split pod in a one-pound jar of sugar. Leave for at least a week (it keeps just fine for months), and the vanilla will permeate the sugar. Use it in baking, mix it into plain yogurt, or sprinkle it on fresh berries.

What Is Vanilla Powder?

Vanilla powder is just that, a powder made from whole ground vanilla beans. It gives you a straight-up vanilla flavor and the nice visual effect of little black dots that's similar to what you see when you use the seeds of a vanilla bean. Make sure you buy **pure unsweetened** vanilla powder—without added sugar. You may have to go to an upscale supermarket to find it, or order it online. It will be more costly than vanilla extract, but you use less. I typically substitute one teaspoon of vanilla powder for two teaspoons of vanilla extract.

VANILLA CRÈME BRÛLÉE

Crème brûlée à la vanille

Classic crème brûlée is a dessert to make the heart wobble. Because there are so few ingredients, you should buy the very best you can—you'll taste the difference. This is a recipe for eight to ten (your guests will thank you). But you can always halve the recipe (let's say for Valentine's Day). You'll have two for dinner and a few for a decadent middle-of-the-night snack…

1⅛ cups whole milk

2 plump vanilla beans

8 egg yolks

¾ cup sugar

3 cups whipping cream
  (30 percent fat)

½ cup turbinado or raw cane
  sugar, to finish

Serves 8 to 10

Preheat the oven to 215°F.

Place the milk in a small saucepan. Split the vanilla beans lengthwise. Lay them flat on a cutting board, seed-side up, and, using the tip of a clean, dry knife, scrape out the sticky seeds and add to the milk. Heat the milk just until boiling, then let cool. (Remember, don't throw away the vanilla pods; put them in a container of sugar to make vanilla sugar!)

In a large mixing bowl, whisk together the egg yolks and sugar until the mixture is a light lemon yellow and the sugar is thoroughly dissolved. Incorporate the cream and the cooled vanilla milk (make sure to use a spatula to get all the vanilla seeds out of the pot). Divide the custard evenly among 8 to 10 shallow ramekins (each about 4 inches in diameter and 1 inch deep). You'll need about ½ cup custard for each ramekin. Bake for 1 hour and 15 minutes until set but still a bit wobbly. Let cool, then refrigerate for at least 3 hours, preferably overnight. Before serving, heat oven to broil and scatter each custard with turbinado sugar. Brown under the broiler for 1 to 2 minutes, just until the sugar melts—you'll want to watch them. Serve immediately. Watch hearts wobble.

Secret #14

Rum and brandy: Few things make a recipe taste more French than a splash of alcohol, so start thinking of your bar as an extension of your pantry. Two essentials: A bottle of brandy or cognac for cooking, and a bottle of rum for baking. I add rum to my crepe batter, clafoutis, and rice pudding. Brandy or sherry is the secret ingredient in my French onion soup. Since I moved to the south, I always have a good bottle of pastis (anise-flavored liqueur) on hand for an *apéro*, but the licorice flavor also makes it an amazing addition to chicken or rabbit stew. I'm not suggesting you break the bank—you don't need to cook with the bottle of 1969 Armagnac that you got for your wedding—but there are plenty of decent midrange brands that will do the trick.

The Fizzy Life

Champagne is less of an ingredient, more of a lifestyle choice. The French know how to live in the moment, and they don't need much of an excuse for a celebration. I always keep a bottle in the cellar for special—and even not-so-special—occasions. (My mother-in-law **loves** champagne—we open a bottle almost every time she comes for the weekend.) Out on the town, champagne is a French woman's best friend: it's elegant and delicious, too expensive to get sloppy drunk on, and won't stain your blouse. Plus it has a lot fewer calories than a strawberry margarita. Good French champagne can be expensive outside of France, so feel free to substitute your favorite dry prosecco, cava, or California sparkling wine. It's the fizz that makes the party!

Cooking with champagne may sound like something out of **Lifestyles of the Rich and Famous,** but if you do happen to have a glass that sits out long enough to go flat, don't throw it away. Add it to the pot just before you puree butternut squash soup, or pour it into the bottom of the casserole dish when you oven-roast fish.

EASY AFTERNOON CREPES

Crêpes sucrées

This is what Gwendal makes for *goûter* when we have friends over. If you have an open kitchen, you can prepare and serve as you go, or you can make a batch in advance, leave them on a plate under a clean tea towel, and serve at room temperature. A generous smear of Nutella is my son's favorite topping. I prefer sugar with a squeeze of lemon—I love the crunch of the grains between my teeth.

7 tablespoons unsalted butter, plus more for cooking

2 cups flour

4 eggs

4¼ cups milk

⅓ cup raw cane sugar or light brown sugar

2 tablespoons best-quality dark rum (or 1 teaspoon orange-flower water or almond essence)

Zest from half a lemon

Makes approximately 16 crepes

In a small saucepan or in the microwave, melt your 7 tablespoons butter and leave to cool.

Meanwhile, in a large mixing bowl, whisk together the flour and the eggs. Slowly add 2 cups milk, whisking thoroughly after each addition to prevent lumps (this is the opposite of pancake batter technique; it's okay to whisk out the lumps). Add the sugar, rum, and lemon zest. Slowly add the remaining milk and butter and whisk to combine. Your finished batter should have the consistency of buttermilk. Let stand for at least half an hour. Like pancake batter, the crepe batter may need to be thinned with a touch more milk just before using; you want it to be very fluid.

Heat a 12-inch nonstick crepe pan over medium-high heat (this takes longer than you might think).

Leave some butter and 3 or 4 clean paper towels by the stove. Get out a ½-cup measure, a large serving plate, and a clean tea towel.

When your crepe pan is nice and hot, add a small pat of butter and wipe it around with a paper towel. (You'll need a pat of butter for every crepe.)

The next part works best with both your hands in action. Holding your scant ½ cup of batter in one hand, pick up the hot crepe pan with the other. Pour the batter in a semicircle toward the sides of the pan, then tilt the pan quickly back and forth until the batter is evenly spread in a very thin layer. Let cook for 1 minute, then run a nonstick spatula under the edges to unstick them. After that, run the spatula all the way around again, this time going about 2 inches under the crepe. By now you should be able to slide the spatula under the center of the crepe. Steady your nerves, and flip. Cook for 30 seconds to 1 minute more. Your crepe will be considerably lighter on the second side, white with brown dots, as opposed to a uniform brown. (Like the first pancake, the first crepe is often a disaster—the pan wasn't hot enough, your mother called while you were flipping, et cetera. Don't worry; this is fun, friendly food—you'll get the hang of it.)

Deliver your finished crepe to a large plate covered with a clean tea towel. To serve, put the crepe flat on your plate, spread half of it with the filling of your choice, and fold. (Kids often fold it again so they can pick up a nice neat triangle.) Devour.

Tip: Never wash that crepe pan! Just wipe it clean when you're done, and it will remain nonstick forever.

Some winning crepe toppings

Sautéed apples and vanilla ice cream

Greek yogurt and raspberry jam

Nutella and bananas

Honey and toasted crushed hazelnuts

Granulated sugar and lemon juice

SIX THINGS
I ALWAYS HAVE IN MY FRIDGE

French fridges are *way* smaller than their American counterparts; the typical French apartment dweller often gets by with a half-fridge that sits under the counter (and a freezer the size of a loaf of Wonder bread). The French shop often—every day for bread, at least once or twice a week for fresh fruit and vegetables. My fridge staples are accents, things I use to make fresh food taste even better.

Just as important as what you will find in a French kitchen is what you will not. When I walk through an American supermarket, I do a little thought experiment; I call it "walk on by." I'm not a nutritionist or a dietitian, but I'm willing to bet a century's worth of croissants that every American could lose five pounds and save fifty bucks a month if he or she just passed by these three items.

Skip the soda: What do the French drink? Water. Not vitamin water, not coconut water, just plain ol' tap water or mineral water. If they're getting fancy, they order a bubbly Perrier. Children do not drink fruit juice (or milk) with meals. Soda is a treat for the kids when they go to a birthday party, or something to provide sugar and fluids when they have *le gastro*, the stomach flu. I don't read a lot of weight-loss books, but one summer my mom gave me a copy of one of the diet books she periodically reads. A phrase jumped off the page, and it's been with me ever since: *People eat because they're thirsty.* I know this has become ubiquitous women's-magazine wisdom, but it's surprising how often we forget to drink. **Proper hydration is one of the central tenets of French womanhood.**

Curb the condiments: I greatly admire Paul Newman, but to me, the salad-dressing aisle remains the greatest mystery of American culinary life. You should see the door of my mother's fridge. There's duck sauce, horseradish sauce, barbecue sauce, oyster sauce, mint jelly, ketchup, three kinds of mustard, and six types of salad dressing, including balsamic vinaigrette (first ingredients: sugar and canola oil), creamy ranch, honey Dijon, and Caesar, all of them so thick with additives that they take away any virtue (or pleasure) a fresh salad might have held. The way forward? Follow that beret! If you concentrate your energy (and budget) on buying high-quality meat, fish, and vegetables, you won't need to cover them up. **The fewer sauces, mixes, and processed foods you buy, the fewer opportunities for disappointing taste and hidden calories.**

Ditch the candy. I love candy. I grew up on Twizzlers, Chuckles, and Hershey's Kisses. For years, the first thing I did when I landed on American soil was buy myself a box of Dots and inhale their chewy corn-syrup comfort on the way home from the airport. (Curiously, twelve hours later I was often in the bathroom vomiting from a migraine.) For whatever reason, I do not eat candy in France. Ever. I didn't think much about this until I saw an article in a French women's magazine about beauty at every age. The section about turning forty began *Fini les regressions*—literally, "Stop regressing." **This is France, so of course you are entitled to your pleasures. Have a glass of wine, get a facial, invest in bars of 70** percent dark chocolate. **But act your age and leave the candy for the kids.** If my seven-year-old wants a *bonbon,* he can go to the local boulangerie, where they sell candy by the piece; each gummy alligator costs five cents. If your kid wants a Twix, let him ride his bike to the corner store, count out his own money, and buy one.

Thank God, there's a loophole. A box of high-quality assorted chocolates is a Christmas treat for the whole family, and we are lucky enough to be invited to an Easter egg hunt every year at our friend Marion's farm (we have to go early or the chocolate eggs melt in the sun). French parents do trot out the candy for kids' birthday parties, often big plastic tubs of Haribo gummy bears, gumdrops, and licorice twists. This is the only occasion I've ever seen a French adult eat candy (and even then, it's one or two, not a handful). My son's preschool teachers used *bonbons* as bribes, but that's another story...

**Secret
#15**

Pork belly/lardons: Everything is better with bacon—I know I've read that somewhere. American chefs have fallen in love with pork belly, which now graces the menus of chic restaurants as a main course. You'll never see the French eating a big chunk of pork belly—too much salt and fat—but they do use it as a base or an accent, often in the form of lardons, little cubes of bacon that find their way into everything from student pasta to coq au vin. My son loves green beans sautéed with lardons; add a baked sweet potato and you have a great weeknight dinner. Lardons remain Gwendal's best cooking trick, a throwback from his student days. He can make dinner out of a package of lardons and almost anything. My favorite is his "risotto of love," which is really just chopped veggies sautéed with lardons and some wild rice cooked with a bouillon cube, all held together with a handful of grated cheese. It's what I want to eat when I'm sick in bed and someone else cooks. I get the warm fuzzies just thinking about it. Lardons are also the base for my favorite quickie pasta sauce—another weeknight favorite.

PENNE WITH CHERRY TOMATOES AND LARDONS

Pâtes aux tomates cerises et lardons fumés

This is delicious—and requires very little prep. You can use regular tomatoes; I just think the whole cherry tomatoes are so pretty in the finished dish. The secret is to cook your pasta al dente, then finish cooking it for a minute or two in the sauce.

2 pounds ripe cherry tomatoes

1 clove garlic

3 tablespoons extra-virgin olive oil

3½ ounces lardons, slab bacon, or pork belly, cut into 1-inch matchsticks

½ teaspoon sugar

¼ teaspoon herbes de Provence or Italian seasoning

Black pepper

½ teaspoon smoked paprika or dried ñora pepper and/or a pinch of hot pepper

⅛ cup white wine

1 pound penne pasta

Fresh basil to garnish

Freshly grated Parmesan cheese

Serves 4

Cut 1 pound of the cherry tomatoes in half; leave the rest whole. Grate the garlic or push it through a garlic press. Put on a big pot of lightly salted water for the pasta.

In a large sauté pan, add the olive oil and brown the lardons until they give off some of their fat, about 5 minutes. Add the tomatoes, garlic, sugar, herbes de Provence, a good grind of black pepper, and the paprika. Simmer over medium-low heat for 3 minutes. Add white wine and simmer for an additional 10 minutes or so, until the sauce thickens up.

Meanwhile, cook 1 pound of penne pasta until al dente. Drain the pasta and add directly to the pot with the sauce. Simmer for 2 minutes, then serve immediately, topped with fresh basil and freshly grated Parmesan.

Dress Up: Add a cup of freshly shelled peas at the end of the recipe, when you combine the pasta and sauce. The crunch adds a lovely contrast of textures.

Secret #16

Fresh herbs: The single biggest change in my daily cooking routine has been the addition of fresh herbs. When I was growing up, we had jars of garlic and onion powder, dried parsley, dried dill, and dried oregano. (When my mother sold the house, thirty years later, I suspect some of those original jars were still in use.) When I moved to Paris, I began buying a bouquet of fresh herbs each week at the outdoor market (my little treat, the way some women buy themselves flowers): fresh bay leaf, thyme, and parsley (for soups and stews), cilantro (for tagines and salads), mint (for fresh mint tea), dill (for fish), and basil (for pasta sauce and homemade pesto). I store my fresh herbs like flowers, their stems in a jar of water, in the door of the fridge. They find their place in almost every dish.

WHOLE-GRAIN SALAD
WITH CHICKPEAS AND HERBS

Salade de petit épeautre aux herbes

This is my go-to salad in the summertime—great for picnics, as a side dish for whatever is on the grill, even as a packed lunch for a long flight. This recipe works really well with quinoa or quick-cooking pearled farro, but I've also found a brand of organic precooked whole grains you can use straight out of the bag. Because there are days when that extra fifteen minutes is the difference between bearable and meltdown.

2 generous cups precooked whole
    grains (quinoa, bulgur, barley,
    farro, or wild rice)

3 tablespoons olive oil

Juice of 1 lemon

1 tablespoon preserved lemon
    (rind only), diced

¼ cup finely chopped cilantro

1 cup finely chopped parsley,
    with stems

Pinch of cinnamon or garam masala

1 16-ounce can chickpeas (or red
    beans), rinsed

Black pepper to taste

*Serves 4
as a side dish*

Cook your grains until slightly al dente. (If you are using quinoa, I find that 1½ cups of water to 1 cup quinoa is the best ratio.) Leave to cool. In a medium mixing bowl, whisk together the olive oil and lemon juice. Add preserved lemon, herbs and spices, chickpeas, and a good grinding of black pepper; toss to combine.

Add the warm grains to the herb mixture; stir to combine. Serve the salad warm, cold, or at room temperature.

Tip: Preserved lemons can be found at Middle Eastern groceries and specialty stores. I use only the outer rind (about a quarter inch thick) and discard the inner pulp. I don't add any salt to this recipe, since preserved lemons are pickled in a salt solution. ***If you can't find the preserved lemons, add a pinch of salt and the zest of ½ lemon instead.***

‹෨ Take a Dip! ෨›

Mint grows like a weed in our garden. Most of it goes to decorate the sundaes at Scaramouche, our ice cream shop, but I'm often plucking a branch here and there for my cooking. I make this yogurt dip at least twice a week during the summer, and it always elicits compliments.

Makes approximately 1½ cups

1 tablespoon freshly squeezed lemon juice

1 tablespoon olive oil

Pinch of coarse sea salt

Grind of black pepper

1 small clove of garlic, finely grated

1 cup whole-milk Greek yogurt (or other strained yogurt)

1 tablespoon sumac (available from Middle Eastern groceries)

¼ cup flat-leaf parsley, finely chopped

2 tablespoons fresh mint leaves, finely chopped

½ small zucchini

In a small mixing bowl, whisk together the lemon juice, olive oil, salt, pepper, and garlic. Add the yogurt and sumac; stir to combine. Add the herbs; stir to combine. Grate the zucchini through the large holes of a cheese grater. (Try to use only the firm outer flesh; cut out the bits in the middle with the seeds.) Stir in the zucchini. Let the dip rest for at least an hour. Serve with crudités or chips, or as a sauce with grilled meat kebabs. It keeps very nicely for a few days in the fridge.

Steamy

It was a rainy afternoon in December the first time Gwendal lured me to his apartment in Paris with the promise of a steaming pot of Moroccan mint tea. He served it in his grandfather's teapot, beaten tin with a graceful spout and an ivory bead at the top so he wouldn't burn his fingers. The rest is history.

To re-create that afternoon, all I need is 2 teaspoons of gunpowder green tea, several sprigs of fresh mint, and 2 or 3 sugar cubes. Put everything in a teapot, cover with boiling water, and let steep for 5 to 7 minutes. Stir, remove the tea and mint, serve.

Secret #17

Plain yogurt: Greek yogurt has made real inroads in the States in the past ten years, so it's a lot easier than it used to be to find a tub of unsweetened yogurt without the insipid fruit compote or raspberry-cheesecake-crumble topping. Plain yogurt with a spoonful of good-quality jam is our go-to dessert or breakfast in the winter, when there are very few fresh fruits. I use plain yogurt as a topping for baked sweet potatoes; as a base (instead of mayo) for my chicken or egg salad; instead of cream cheese or sour cream for dip (see Take a Dip!, page 60); and, of course, to make yogurt cake, which remains one of my favorite things ever to emerge from a French kitchen.

CLASSIC YOGURT CAKE

Gâteau au yaourt

This is the first cake most French children learn to bake; they measure the ingredients straight out of the rinsed yogurt pot. I've been toying with my recipe for years now. This version is my latest winner—my son recently had three pieces for his *goûter*. He told me it was super-super-super-*sympa*. Anything that gets three *super*s is a keeper.

1½ cups flour

Pinch of fine sea salt

1 teaspoon baking powder

1 teaspoon baking soda

1¼ cups sugar

Zest of 1 lemon

3 eggs

½ cup vegetable oil (I use olive oil!)

1 cup plain whole-milk yogurt

Serves 6 to 8

Preheat your oven to 350°F. Line a 10-inch springform pan or ceramic tart mold with a sheet of waxed paper.

In a small bowl, combine flour, salt, baking powder, and baking soda.

In a medium bowl, combine sugar and lemon zest. Add the eggs and whisk until the mixture is a light lemon yellow. Add oil and yogurt; whisk thoroughly to combine. Add the flour mixture and whisk to combine. Pour the butter into the prepared pan.

Bake for 35 to 40 minutes, until well browned on top and a toothpick comes out clean. Cool on a rack, then unmold and cool completely. It keeps well for 2 to 3 days wrapped in aluminum foil. Trust me, it won't last that long.

Try this

Yogurt cake is also great for cupcakes.

Bake at 350°F for 18 to 20 minutes (makes about 15 medium

cupcakes). Serve plain in a lunch box, with raspberry jam for

brunch, or with your favorite frosting for a birthday party.

Yogurt cake is very forgiving; it actually gets better with age.

You can make these up to two days in advance.

Add mini–chocolate chips to the batter if you like, or top

with fresh raspberries, but before you start getting fancy with

the additions, I advise you to try it the French way—plain.

**Secret
#18**

Cheese: There is no overestimating the importance of cheese in the French diet—in the French conception of self, really. But not just any cheese. Raw-milk, oozy, stinky, drenched in alcohol or covered in mold—all this is considered a uniquely French bit of heaven. Ask a Frenchman abroad what he misses most, and the likely answer is some version of *Camembert au lait cru*. The French serve cheese between the main course and dessert (sometimes instead of dessert). If you are cooking the French way, you are making limited amounts for the main course, so a small wedge of cheese at the end of the meal is a welcome (sometimes necessary) addition. A hunk of Comté and baguette is a favorite snack when we'll be eating late and my son wants something before dinner. A lightly dressed green salad topped with some lardons and a tartine of toasted sourdough and warm goat cheese is a full meal.

Wondering why traditional family meals in France (quiches, gratins, croque-monsieurs) often contain large doses of dairy? Kids in France do not drink milk as a beverage (unless you count their morning hot chocolate). Cheese, cream, and yogurt provide the majority of their calcium.

WARM GOAT CHEESE SALAD

Salade de chèvre chaud

After all these years, this stands as my perfect French meal—so much more than the sum of its parts. It's great for a group of friends when you want to spend less time making lunch, more time in the garden with a bottle of rosé.

1 large head frisée lettuce

3 tomatoes, cut into eighths

1 tablespoon olive oil

¾ pound lardons (pork belly or slab bacon cut into ¼-inch-by-1-inch cubes)

6 slices whole-grain bread, each about ½ inch thick

6 individual goat cheeses (3 ounces each)

Drizzle of honey

Double recipe of My Favorite French Vinaigrette (page 11)

Serves 6

Preheat the oven to 400°F.

Wash and dry the lettuce; set aside. Place tomatoes in a small bowl.

In a large frying pan, heat the olive oil and brown the lardons. Turn off the heat, remove the lardons with a slotted spoon, and mix them with the tomatoes. Take each slice of bread and press into the bacon fat, turning to coat both sides. Leave the slices of bread in the pan, cover, and let rest for a few minutes; this allows the bread to steam a bit, so it's less likely to dry out when you put it in the oven with the cheese. Line a cookie sheet with aluminum foil. Cut each round of goat cheese in half horizontally, so you've got 2 disks. Lay 2 disks of cheese on each piece of bread; drizzle with honey.

Bake on the center rack for 12 to 15 minutes, until the goat cheese is heated through.

While the toasts are in the oven, put 2 tablespoons of dressing in the bottom of a large salad bowl, add the lettuce, toss to coat, and taste. Add a bit more dressing if you like, but don't drown things. Mix in the tomatoes and lardons. Divide the salad among 6 plates. Put the goat-cheese toasts on top. Serve immediately.

⋙ Vive la Tartine! ⋘

Looking for a way to minimize the bread in your favorite sandwich? During lunch hour at a French bistro, you might see the waiter rush by with a flattish open-faced sandwich called a tartine, along with a large green salad. There are endless variations: Toast a large thin piece of sourdough bread and top it with smoked salmon and arugula, tomato and avocado, cheese and prosciutto, or ricotta and grilled veggies, to name a few. Unlike a sandwich, this is not finger food—the French eat their tartines with a knife and fork!

Eat the fat

The French are not afraid of fat. Like everything else,
it's meant to be eaten in moderation and appreciated for its
taste and texture. I use 2 percent or whole-milk yogurt, since
nonfat simply doesn't have the taste or texture to hold up in
*cooking. And—**quelle horreur**—let's not even talk about low-fat*
cheese; de Gaulle is rolling over in his grave. The French would
rather eat a pinkie-size slice of fruity Comté or
creamy chèvre than a whole pack of flavorless
fat-free string cheese.

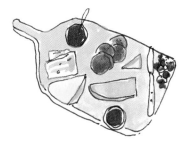

**Secret
#19**

Eggs: I use a lot of eggs in France—poached eggs with steamed asparagus, fried eggs on top of buckwheat crepes, lightly beaten eggs for quiche filling, and, of course, all that baking. Since I often eat eggs less than fully cooked, I make sure to buy organic or, now that we live in the country, from someone I know at my local outdoor market.

ENDIVE, PEAR, AND ROQUEFORT SALAD WITH CURED HAM AND A POACHED EGG

*Salade endive, poire,
Roquefort avec jambon cru et œuf pochée*

When I'm on my own, I often make meals that are more like arts and crafts projects than actual cooking. I love slicing and stacking, artfully arranging. Bitter endive, creamy blue cheese, and sweet pears are a classic French salad; two slices of cured ham and a silky poached egg on top make this into one of my favorite solo meals.

1 Belgian endive, cut lengthwise
   into eighths

½ Bosc pear, cut into eighths

3 thin slices of Roquefort blue cheese

2 slices of cured ham (such as
   prosciutto)

Walnut or olive oil

Sherry vinegar

1 organic or free-range egg

Black pepper

Serves 1

Stack the endive and pear on a plate. Top with blue cheese (leaving space in the center for the egg). Arrange slices of ham around the sides of the plate. Drizzle with walnut oil and a very small amount of vinegar.

Fill a small saucepan halfway with water and put over medium heat. Crack your egg into a small bowl. When the water begins to simmer, lower the heat and gently slide the egg from the bowl into the water. Simmer for 3 minutes. Carefully remove the egg with a slotted spoon to drain. Place the egg on top of the salad. Add a grind of fresh pepper and enjoy!

‎❧ Out of the Pantry, into the Sublime ❧

There are certain ingredients that completely transform themselves from one culture to another. I've had several religious experiences in my discovery of French cuisine, but none more profound than my first taste of homemade mayonnaise. For the French, mayo isn't something that sits in a jar on the door of the fridge awaiting a tuna fish sandwich; it's a silky, golden sauce, prepared fresh each time it's eaten. Truth be told, I used to despise mayonnaise. I spent my entire childhood avoiding anything stuck between two pieces of bread so I wouldn't have to risk contact with the slimy white goo. Then came that revelatory Sunday, my first lunch with Gwendal's parents: steamed cod, leeks, and red potatoes—served with homemade mayonnaise. I watched my future mother-in-law beat the egg yolks with a pinch of salt, a dab of Dijon, and a steady trickle of oil. I didn't *want* to taste it, but I was raised better than that. I gingerly spread the smallest possible amount on my cod. And then—the heavens opened and the angels sang.

French mayonnaise is made with raw eggs, which tends to scare Americans—and, I've since learned, with good reason. Many chickens in the U.S. are raised in abominable conditions. As a result, eggs are consistently washed, which removes some of the natural protections built into the shell. (That's why eggs are stored in the refrigerated section of a U.S. supermarket; in France, you'll find them at room temperature on the shelves.) That said, if you are willing to buy the freshest organic eggs and try this once, you'll never look at baked cod, crab legs, deviled eggs, or steamed cauliflower quite the same way again.

⸈ Homemade Mayonnaise ⸋

The key to success is to have everything, from the bowl to the eggs, at room temperature.

1 egg yolk (only the freshest organic egg; remember, you're eating it raw)
1 tablespoon Dijon mustard
Scant ¼ teaspoon coarse sea salt
½ cup safflower, sunflower, peanut, or other mild vegetable oil

Combine egg yolk, mustard, and salt in a small mixing bowl. Using an electric egg beater, beat the yolk mixture while adding a few drops of oil at a time. When the mixture begins to thicken and set, add a tiny but steady trickle of oil. The mayonnaise will not take more than a minute or two to puff up.

It's never happened to me, but apparently there are days when the mayonnaise just won't take. Old wives' tales abound—I was once told a woman shouldn't make mayonnaise when she has her period! There's no magic in this recipe; just add the oil drop by drop at the beginning to make sure the emulsion holds.

You can use a mild-tasting olive oil if you like—that and the addition of raw garlic and a squeeze of lemon juice will elevate a simple mayonnaise to the French *aïoli*.

Pregnant women and anyone with an allergy to raw eggs are advised not to eat this.

Makes about ½ cup

**Secret
#20**

Anchovies: I like Nigella Lawson's take on anchovies—"a little white lie never hurt anyone." People *think* they don't like anchovies—too strong, too fishy—so why announce your secret ingredient? Just watch your guests' faces light up when they taste the salty, savory goodness of a simple pasta dish (olive oil, parsley, chopped anchovies, and black olives) or a fabulous dip for raw vegetables (pureed anchovies, olive oil, and basil). Anchovies (along with mounds of sautéed onions) are the topping on my favorite Provençal pizza, *la pissaladière*.

SIMPLE SPAGHETTI WITH ANCHOVIES

Spaghettis aux anchois

Gwendal and I love Italy. But since we founded Scaramouche, our artisan ice cream business, we work all summer, so vacations are few and far between. This rustic pasta dish makes me feel like I'm on holiday and uses just a few pantry staples.

¼ cup olive oil

½ cup finely chopped flat-leaf parsley

5 large cloves garlic, finely grated or pushed through a garlic press

6 anchovies packed in olive oil (I buy the spicy ones if available), plus 4 to 5 additional anchovies, finely chopped

5 or 6 cured black olives, pitted and chopped

2 large pinches of oregano

1 teaspoon smoked pepper flakes (such as ñora pepper) or ¼ teaspoon smoked paprika

1 pound spaghetti

1 cup tomatoes, chopped

Red pepper flakes, for serving

Serves 4

Combine olive oil, parsley, garlic, 6 anchovies, olives, oregano, and 1 teaspoon pepper flakes to make a chunky paste. I suppose you could do this in the food processor, but I like the rougher texture I get when I do it by hand.

Transfer the anchovy paste to a large frying pan. Bring a stockpot of lightly salted water to a boil. Add the spaghetti and cook until al dente. While the spaghetti is cooking, heat the anchovy paste, stirring continuously for about 3 minutes, until the garlic starts to give off that wonderful smell. Turn off the heat. Drain the spaghetti, then quickly add to frying pan with the warm anchovy paste. Toss well to coat. Add the remaining chopped anchovies and the tomatoes. Toss to combine. Serve immediately with red pepper flakes.

Deep Freeze

*There are a few things I always keep in my freezer for a rainy day: good sausages for a big pot of lentils, frozen tart crusts and puff pastry, and a couple of bags of raw shrimp and baby scallops (I never buy cooked frozen shrimp; they just get soggy) for stir-fry. I keep a few packages of lardons for emergencies (e.g., Sundays, when the shops are closed) and slabs of pork belly for my split-pea soup. I have a small family, and I don't like to see the same food two days in a row, so my freezer is full of **les restes** (that's French for "leftovers"). I'm always happy to eat lentils again in a week or two without the additional prep.*

FRUITS AND VEGETABLES

In France, a love of seasonal fruits and vegetables is not a foodie fad; it cuts across all classes and regions. There's a certain pride in the building blocks of everyday life. The French are simply closer to their land—and thus to their food—than we are. Weekly outdoor markets remain an institution in almost every town and village. Everyone seems to have a relative with a house in the country where there are tomato vines or a pear tree in the garden. Gwendal has strong memories of stomachaches from eating too many blackberries when he went out picking for his grandmother's jam.

In the States, your local farmers' market is your best bet for finding seasonal produce. You'll see what really came out of the ground that week, instead of what was flown in from Chile. It's a fun Saturday-morning outing, plus you'll be supporting the local economy—and it might be closer than your nearest Trader Joe's.

Secret #21

Zucchini flowers: Few things will delight your guests more than eating a flower! These sunny yellow blooms are the very essence of seasonal cooking: a fleeting summer treat. Serve warm in the garden with a glass of rosé or, better yet, a bottle of pastis!

Buy your zucchini flowers at the farmers' market in the morning and store them in the fridge like a bouquet—with the stems in a glass of cold water—until you are ready to use them.

ZUCCHINI BLOSSOMS WITH GOAT CHEESE, FRESH MINT, AND ANISE SEEDS

*Fleurs de courgettes farcies au chèvre, à la menthe,
et aux graines d'anis*

I've made lots of variations of this recipe over the years (chervil and sun-dried tomatoes, fresh dill and cumin seeds), but this is the one that I keep coming back to. The flavors are lively but not so strong that they overpower the delicate taste of the flowers themselves.

1 egg

6 ounces soft goat cheese, cut into small cubes

1 teaspoon whole anise seeds

1½ tablespoons chopped fresh mint

Pinch of coarse sea salt

Freshly ground black pepper

12 large zucchini blossoms

1 tablespoon olive oil

*Serves 4 as hors d'oeuvres or
a light appetizer*

Preheat the oven to 350°F.

In a small bowl, lightly beat the egg. Add the cheese, anise seeds, mint, salt, and pepper and mash/mix with a fork to combine. Carefully hold open each flower (no need to remove the stamen, but do check for ants) and stuff with a heaping teaspoon of filling. (Depending on the size of your zucchini blossoms, you may have a bit of stuffing left over.) Twist the ends of the flowers to close. Place the olive oil in a 9-by-13-inch casserole dish and shake it around so it coats the entire bottom of the dish. Gently roll each zucchini flower in the oil and retwist the ends to make sure they're closed.

Bake for 20 minutes, until fragrant and golden. Serve immediately. These are not quite finger food; you'll need a small plate and a fork to eat them.

Try this

If I have half a cup of quinoa
or wild rice left over from dinner, I'll throw it
into the cheese mixture and make double
the number of blossoms.

**Secret
#22**

Celery root: Behold, your new favorite mashed pota-toes. This hairy beige bowling ball of a vegetable is the very reason your mother told you never to judge a book by its cover. Although celery root may look like Franken-stein's brain, it is among my favorite French discoveries. You won't believe it till you try it, but this will satisfy your longing for a big heap of smooth buttery comfort without the stodgy feeling of a Thanksgiving Day food coma.

CELERY ROOT MASH

Purée de céleri

3½ pounds celery root (1 large
    or 2 small), peeled and
    chopped into 1-inch cubes

2 to 3 tablespoons olive oil

1 medium onion

½ teaspoon garam masala

1½ to 2 cups chicken or
    vegetable broth

Butter, if broiling (optional)

Serves 4, generously

In a stockpot fitted with a metal colander, steam celery root until tender. Discard the cooking water and set the celery root aside.

In the same stockpot, heat the olive oil and sauté the onion with the garam masala for 5 minutes, until the onion is translucent. Return the celery root to the pot and sauté together over low heat for 3 or 4 minutes more. Add the chicken broth and puree with a hand blender. At first it will seem too thick to puree, but keep at it. I resist adding more chicken broth (I'm a perfectionist in so many other aspects of my life, I don't need to get obsessive about lumps), but the final consistency is up to you. Serve at once or put in a gratin dish, dot with butter, and place under the broiler for a minute or two. This is great with meat but light enough to serve with fish as well.

Variation: Mix in chopped dill or chervil or a handful of freshly grated Parmesan just before serving.

Secret #23

Leeks: My childhood memories of leeks extend no further than a six-inch white stub sold under plastic in the ShopRite "soup pack." In France, leeks are everywhere. They are among the first vegetables given to kids, and the French eat a lot of them in the winter (there's not much else on offer). I like them sautéed with olive oil and a hint of Dijon mustard (see page 13). Leeks are grown-up nursery food; they are a mild base for soup and a perfect side for baked cod or chicken breast. Leek and bacon quiche is a classic combo for a weekday supper or a weekend brunch.

LEEK AND BACON QUICHE

Tarte aux poireaux et aux lardons

I'm not a fan of soggy crust, and prebaking is just too much work for a weeknight, so I've improvised a gluten-free version of this quiche, made with a layer of toasted almond flour at the bottom. Like the crushed-cookie crust of a cheesecake, the almond flour firms up in the oven. By all means, if you are cooking this for company, take the time to make a homemade pastry crust, prebake it, add the filling, and cook as directed.

4 medium leeks; you should have a little over 1 pound when trimmed

8 ounces lardons, pork belly, or slab bacon, cut into small cubes

1 cup almond flour

5 eggs

½ cup crème fraîche or whipping cream (30 percent fat)

¾ cup milk

2 teaspoons Dijon mustard

¼ teaspoon coarse sea salt

Freshly ground black pepper

1 cup grated Gruyère cheese

Serves 6

Preheat the oven to 350°F. Line a 10-inch springform pan with waxed paper. Wash and trim the leeks. You want just the white and light green bits, so cut off the hairy bottom and the dark green leaves on top. You should have just over 1 pound left. Cut the leeks into ¼-inch rounds.

In a large frying pan, sauté lardons until they give off some fat, about 5 minutes. Remove with a slotted spoon. Add leeks to the hot fat in the pan and sauté for 10 minutes, until wilted. Meanwhile, toast the almond flour in a dry frying pan until golden, stirring often to avoid overbrowning.

In a large bowl, whisk together eggs, crème fraîche, milk, mustard, salt, and a good grind of black pepper. Add half the cheese and whisk to combine.

Spread your almond flour evenly over the bottom of the pan. Scatter the lardons over the almond flour, followed by the leeks. Gently pour in the egg/cheese mixture. Top with the remaining cheese. Bake for 40 minutes, until set but slightly wobbly in the center. Cool on a rack for 15 minutes. Unmold from the pan and serve warm with a big green salad.

Try this

There's a single-serving stovetop version of this dish that I sometimes make for lunch: Chop 1 leek into ¼-inch rounds. Boil for 1 minute and drain. Meanwhile, fry 2 strips of bacon in a small omelet pan. Remove the bacon, add the leeks to the bacon fat, and stir. Cook for 3 minutes, until the water from the leeks has evaporated. Meanwhile, lightly mix 2 or 3 eggs in a bowl. Put the bacon back in the pan, pour the eggs on top, reduce the heat to low, and cover tightly. Leave for 2 or 3 minutes, until the eggs are set. If they are not set by then, just cover the pan again, turn off the heat, and wait a bit.

Leek Detox

After too much foie gras, champagne, and chocolate over Christmas, a French woman's New Year's resolutions might include a *régime de poireaux*—a few days of light lunches and leek soup for dinner. Leeks are low in calories and a natural diuretic, so they help reduce that post-holiday bloat. Here's a basic recipe: Slice and steam 4 leeks (white and light green parts only) in 2 cups water plus 2 cups broth until tender. Cook 1 cubed potato in the liquid you used to steam the leeks. Combine the liquid, potato, and leeks and puree until smooth (keep blending until there are no stringy bits).

It's Personal

The very first morning in our new home in Céreste, our neighbor Jeannot left a basket of tomatoes, zucchini, and eggplants from his garden on the doorstep; he stopped by later that day to instruct me on how to make zucchini soup for the baby. The fishmonger at the Thursday market knows better than Immigration how long I spend in the States—if I don't come to buy dorade for three weeks in a row, he starts asking questions. If my husband buys a baguette in the morning and I pass by the boulangerie before lunch, the baker's wife will wave me away— *"Monsieur est déjà venu."* My food in France is not something anonymous, sold under cellophane. There's a person behind almost everything I eat. The French know this is not about snobbery—it's about humanity.

Secret #24

Swiss chard: *Blettes* is not a sexy word, even in French. It sounds like *blah, blech.* Generally not good. But since I arrived in Provence, Swiss chard has become my new favorite vegetable. Lightly sautéed with olive oil, it makes a quick side dish; it's slightly sweet and doesn't give off a lot of water, so it's a great substitute for spinach in quiche. As with kale (which the French have yet to truly embrace), the texture of raw Swiss chard holds up really well, so when I travel (airline food—*non, merci*), I'll pack a chicken breast and shred some Swiss chard to put under some version of my chickpea salad (page 58). I know the chard won't get soggy even when dressed in advance.

When we first arrived in Provence, I heard about a dessert from Nice called *tourte aux blettes,* made with Swiss chard, apples, pine nuts, and raisins, and topped with powdered sugar. I love sweet and savory combinations, so I decided to turn this into a kind of dinner pie, with an olive oil herb crust and a handful of Parmesan thrown in. If you are in love with a vegetarian, or just having one over for Thanksgiving, this is what you should make—though the turkey eaters will be fighting for a slice as well.

SWISS CHARD PIE WITH APPLES, RAISINS, AND PINE NUTS

Tourte aux blettes

For the crust

- 2⅔ cups flour
- 2 tablespoons sugar
- ¼ teaspoon fine sea salt
- ¼ teaspoon herbes de Provence
- ½ cup olive oil
- ¼ cup plus 2 tablespoons ice water
- 1 tablespoon milk

Serves 4 as a main dish,
8 as a side

For the filling

- ¼ cup pine nuts
- 2 tablespoons sultanas or golden raisins
- 1 tablespoon olive oil
- 1 pound Swiss chard, finely chopped
- ½ cup freshly grated Parmesan cheese
- 1 tablespoon flour
- 2 pinches of cinnamon
- 2 pinches of nutmeg
- 2 small sweet/tart apples (such as Braeburn or Cortland)
- Squeeze of lemon juice

To make the crust: Combine flour, sugar, salt, and herbes de Provence in a large mixing bowl, then make a well in the flour mixture and add oil. Cut together using two knives until the mixture resembles coarse crumbs. Slowly add water and stir just until the ingredients are combined and the dough comes together; do not overwork. Separate dough into two balls, cover with plastic wrap, and refrigerate for at least 30 minutes (you can make the crust the night before, if you like).

While the crust is resting, brown the pine nuts over low heat in a small frying pan. Watch them so they don't burn. Combine with the sultanas or raisins and set aside.

In a large sauté pan, heat olive oil and add Swiss chard. Sauté over medium heat for 5 to 6 minutes. Remove to a colander to drain.

Preheat your oven to 400°F. Take out a 10-inch tart pan or pie plate.

In a small mixing bowl, toss the freshly grated Parmesan with the flour, cinnamon, and nutmeg.

Thinly slice apples into a large mixing bowl and toss them with a squeeze of fresh lemon juice to prevent oxidation.

Now roll out your bottom crust to about 14 inches. You'll want to do this between two sheets of waxed paper so you won't have to add any flour. Take off the top sheet of waxed paper and use the bottom one to flip your crust into the pan. Prick the crust with a fork.

Add the Swiss chard, pine nuts, and raisins to the bowl with the apples and toss to combine. Then add the cheese/flour/spice mixture and toss to combine.

Roll out your top crust using the same method, between two pieces of waxed paper. Fill the pie with the Swiss chard mixture. Flip the crust on top and crimp the edges together (I like to leave the edges rustic and thick, rather than trimming them—more crispy crust for me!). Make 4 or 5 slashes in the top of the pie. Brush the crust with the tablespoon of milk.

Bake on the center rack for 15 minutes at 400°F, then lower the heat to 350°F and bake for 25 minutes more, until golden brown. Serve warm from the oven.

❧ Real Food, Not Super-food ❧

I feel like every time I go to the States, there's a new super-food—kale, goji berries, hemp, algae—that I'm supposed to be eating. The French eat a wide variety of whole foods, but they are not looking for a silver bullet, a single ingredient that will prevent cancer or make someone lose twenty pounds in two weeks.

In France, good food has always been the best medicine. What is a health fad in the States might be age-old wisdom in France. Ask French people why they feed their kids leeks or eat lentils for dinner (with a glass of red wine, of course), and they will not ramble on about antioxidants. They're likely to say, *"C'est comme ça"*— meaning that's how they've always done it. It's tradition, not science. If a "recent study" happens to confirm it's a good idea, so much the better (insert Gallic shrug here). You're not telling them anything their grandmothers didn't already know.

Secret #25

Fresh figs: In the fifteen years I've been in France, few ingredients have added more pleasure to my life than fresh figs. When we first moved to Céreste, our babysitter let us in on a little secret: There is a public fig tree behind the post office. It's still popular enough that it's hard to get there before the figs are gone, but that's my kind of public service! Fresh figs are a coy fruit; the dusky purple teardrops don't look like much, but break one open and you'll find a pulpy kaleidoscope of seeds. A ripe fig should give a little when you pinch it, like the cheeks of a well-fed child. You can use them in sweet or savory recipes, in appetizers or desserts, or tossed in salads as a textural treat.

FIG AND ALMOND TART
WITH TOASTED PINE NUTS

Tarte aux figues et aux pignons de pins

Happily, entertaining these days can be a collective affair. One person might be responsible for pre-dinner nibbles, another might be asked to bring dessert. This rustic fruit tart is often my contribution. It can be made with any seasonal fruit—pears, apricots, or plums—but there's something unexpected, and rather grand, about the duet of fresh figs and pine nuts. The secret is the rum-spiked frangipane (French almond cream) which is the basis of any self-respecting tart.

For the crust

This quick one-pot pastry recipe is from our friend Anne. I've also made this tart without the crust; the almond cream gets crisp underneath. Just line a metal tart or cake pan with a sheet of waxed paper.

9 tablespoons butter
4 tablespoons water
1 tablespoon sugar
1¾ cups flour

In a small saucepan, combine butter, water, and sugar. When the butter is melted, stir thoroughly to combine. When the mixture is just about to simmer, turn off the heat and add the flour all at once, stirring with a wooden spoon to combine. Roll out the crust with a rolling pin until it is about 13 inches in diameter.

For the filling

7 tablespoons salted butter
  (if you can find it with sea-salt crystals,
  so much the better)

½ cup plus 2 tablespoons granulated sugar

3 eggs

1 tablespoon dark rum

½ teaspoon almond extract or a few
  drops of real bitter almond essence

½ teaspoon vanilla extract

1½ cups almond flour

6 or 7 ripe fresh figs sliced
  about ⅓ inch thick

Small handful of pine nuts

2 tablespoons powdered sugar

Serves 8

Heat the oven to 375°F.

Whip the butter until soft and airy. Add the sugar, and cream the two together until light and fluffy. Add two eggs; whisk to combine.

Break the third egg into a cup; stir lightly. Pour half of the third egg into the batter. Put the cup with the remaining half egg to one side. Add the rum and almond and vanilla extracts to the batter; whisk to combine. Add the almond flour and stir to combine.

Place the crust in an 11-inch tart pan (preferably a metal tart pan with a removable bottom or a springform pan—the metal helps the crust cook through). Let the extra crust hang over the edges. Prick the bottom of the crust with a fork. Top with the almond cream. Place the sliced figs on top. Scatter on the pine nuts. Fold the extra crust over the top of the tart to form a little border. Mix the remaining half egg with the powdered sugar and brush the top of the folded-over crust with the egg wash.

Bake for 30 to 35 minutes, until golden and cooked through.

Try this

Roasted figs with creamy blue cheese and honey

can do double duty. They make lovely hors d'oeuvres, or you

can serve them after dinner with a green salad—a combination

of cheese course and dessert. Take 8 perfectly ripe figs, cut them in

half, then drizzle with a tablespoon of olive oil and a bit of honey.

Roast in a 350°F oven for 15 minutes, until tender. Remove from

the oven and top each fig with a small piece of Roquefort, Stilton,

or Gorgonzola. Serve immediately with a handful of arugula salad.

Serves 4 as an appetizer or cheese course

❧ Can It! ❧

Summer in Provence doesn't leave a lot of room for free will. July and August are an avalanche of apricots, peaches, zucchini, and, quite simply the best tomatoes I've ever tasted. Now I know what women in Provence were doing all day before YouTube: they were canning and preserving the summer bounty for a long cold winter. I haven't mastered my canning technique yet, so at the height of the season I freeze bags of fresh-shelled peas and cranberry beans, apricot compote and ratatouille. I also make batch after batch of these garlic-roasted tomatoes. Finding a container of these beauties at the bottom of the freezer in January is like Christmas all over again. I use them as a simple pasta sauce or with white wine as a base for braised veal or lamb. Bake them in a pie dish with a puff pastry crust on top, then flip the whole thing, and you have instant tomato tarte tatin!

What you'll need:

4 pounds perfect heirloom tomatoes, sliced 1 inch thick

1 head garlic

A few sprigs fresh thyme

$1/3$ cup extra-virgin olive oil

Coarse sea salt to taste

1 teaspoon sugar

Heat the oven to 325°F. Line your largest baking sheet with aluminum foil. Arrange the sliced tomatoes in a single layer, tuck the cloves of garlic (unpeeled) and the thyme between them, and pour the olive oil over all. Sprinkle with a pinch or two of coarse sea salt and the sugar. Bake for 1½ to 2 hours, until the garlic is tender and the tomatoes are soft and a bit wrinkly. When everything has cooled a bit, remove the garlic from its peel; this should be easy to do with your fingers. If not using immediately, carefully layer the tomatoes and garlic in a shallow container, keeping as many whole as you can. Don't forget to pour in every last drop of that tomato liquid. For the last slick of oil, wipe your cookie sheet with a slice of bread. A well-earned snack for the cook!

Store in the fridge for a day or two or freeze for a snowy day.

MEAT AND FISH

The French love a cute dog in a handbag as much as anyone—but they are also pragmatic and utterly unsentimental about eating animals. Until very recently, our house in Céreste had more space for livestock than for humans. There was once a donkey in our cellar, and our bedroom is a refinished hayloft where the former residents used to hang the cured hams. Maybe it's the closeness to their agricultural past, or the memory of the scarcity of the war years, but in France, *nothing* goes to waste. Fish heads make great soup, and you are as likely to find kidneys or blood sausage on a French table as a filet mignon.

**Secret
#26**

Whole fish: Americans are always in search of quick fixes, fifteen-minute meals. I know whole fish doesn't sound like fast food, but it is. The protective skin makes high-heat methods, like broiling or grilling, a real option. They also look splendid on the plate—head, tail, and all. I discovered whole fish because I had to; the fishmonger at my Tuesday market in Belleville didn't sell fillets. Gutting my first mackerel over the kitchen sink in Paris gave me a primitive thrill. Who knew there was such a cavewoman lurking beneath my ladylike façade? If you can't find whole fish at your local supermarket, try an Asian supermarket; they often sell them right out of the tank.

BROILED SEA BREAM WITH LEMON AND HERBS

Dorade au citron et aux herbes

This method works well with any small whole fish. You can vary the herbs to suit your taste or use lime or orange slices instead of lemon.

4 sea bream, 9 to 11 ounces each,
   gutted and scales rubbed off

1 tablespoon olive oil

Sea salt

2 slices lemon, cut in half

Fresh parsley, thyme, dill, or other herbs

Serves 4

Preheat your oven to broil. Put a double layer of foil on a cookie sheet.

Lay out your fish; drizzle with oil. Rub the oil all over the fish, including tails and heads. Sprinkle each cavity with a pinch of sea salt and stuff each with half a lemon slice and herbs.

Position your cookie sheet on the highest rack, about 2 inches from the heat. Broil fish for 5 or 6 minutes, or until the skin bubbles and chars in a few spots. Don't worry if the fins stick straight up and burn a bit. Turn carefully; you'll need a spatula and a fork for this operation. Cook for 2 to 3 minutes more. You can tell if the fish is done by inserting the tip of a small knife next to the bone; if the fillet is opaque and pulls away easily, it's ready. Always err on the side of caution. It's better to undercook slightly and put it back than to ruin a perfect piece of fish by overcooking it.

Secret #27

Braising cuts: French cooks are often frugal as well as creative. They know that a tough gelatinous beef cheek or oxtail will, after a few hours in the oven, yield something sublime. *Échine de porc* (shoulder pork butt) is just about the cheapest cut of meat available at my butcher. It's also one of the tastiest; marbled with fat, it cooks up tender—almost melting in the pot. My mother-in-law makes a simple version of this dish with French beer, onions, and paprika, but we have many Belgian neighbors in Céreste, so I've taken to substituting Belgian beer and adding vinegar, brown sugar, and Dijon mustard in the style of a *carbonnade flamande*. This is the dinner I want after a day of sledding or skiing; it warms me to the core. Like most braised dishes, it can be made ahead of time; it tastes even better the next day.

SLOW-COOKED PORK BUTT WITH BEER

Échine de porc à la bière

2 tablespoons olive oil

4 pounds shoulder pork butt, cut into
6 thick slices

Coarse sea salt

Freshly ground black pepper

2 large onions, halved and sliced

1 tablespoon flour or cornstarch

2 tablespoons sherry vinegar or
red wine vinegar

1 heaping tablespoon turbinado (raw)
sugar, or 1 tablespoon packed
light brown sugar

3 cups Belgian beer, such as Leffe Blond

2 cloves

A few sprigs of fresh thyme

2 tablespoons Dijon mustard

Serves 6

Preheat the oven to 350°F.

In a large Dutch oven with a tight-fitting lid, heat 1 tablespoon olive oil. Brown the meat, seasoning with salt and pepper as you go. Remove the meat and set aside.

Heat the remaining tablespoon of olive oil in the Dutch oven; add the onions and sauté until lightly colored, 3 to 5 minutes. Sprinkle the onions with flour or cornstarch; stir to coat. Add the vinegar and sugar; stir to combine. Pour in the beer, then add the meat, meat juices, cloves, and thyme to the pot. Stir in the Dijon mustard. The sauce will not completely cover the meat.

Cook, tightly covered, in the oven for 1 hour. Remove from the oven and turn the meat, submerging any pieces that did not get a chance to soak up the sauce in the first hour. Return the pot to the oven for 1 hour. Remove from the oven and cool completely (push the meat to one side so the sauce forms a puddle; this makes it easier to skim the fat later). When cold (I sometimes leave my Le Creuset outside on a windowsill all night), skim the fat from the sauce. Reheat and serve in shallow bowls with steamed carrots and lots of egg noodles to soak up the sauce.

⁓ The Juicy Bits ⁓

In Céreste, a trip to the butcher on Saturday morning might take an hour, but by the time I make my way to the register to pay, I've gotten not only my lamb shoulder, *pâté au piment d'espelette,* and pork belly, but every last piece of village gossip worth having. Even with the rise of *hypermarchés*—giant American-style supermarkets—the butcher remains an important local figure. Mine is at once alluring and reassuring, like having a cute doctor. He gives me the confidence to try new things, like rabbit, which I would never buy under cellophane. I can be sure of the quality I'm getting, and he always has tips on how to prepare the meat. Butchers, at least in France, tend to have a saucy sense of humor. Go for the meat, return for the banter.

⁓ Rabbit with Cider and Honey ⁓
Lapin au cidre

This is the first rabbit recipe I ever made, a rite of passage for any American. The spike of the cider and mellow sweetness of the honey are perfect complements to the slight gaminess of the meat. This is easy enough for a weekend dinner, festive enough for a holiday meal; I made it instead of turkey for my first Parisian Thanksgiving. If your family is not quite ready for rabbit, try this with a good-quality chicken instead.

1½ tablespoons butter

3 tablespoons olive oil

1 rabbit, cut in 6 pieces, with the liver

Coarse sea salt

Freshly ground black pepper

2 carrots, roughly chopped

4 ounces fresh pearl onions, whole (or 4 shallots, coarsely chopped)

1 stalk celery, roughly chopped

1 clove garlic, whole

1 tablespoon Calvados (or applejack)

1 cup hard cider (the drier, the better)

1 bouquet garni (thyme, parsley, bay leaf)

2 tablespoons honey

¼ cup crème fraîche or whipping cream (30 percent fat)

Fresh chervil to garnish

In a large frying pan, heat the butter and oil. Brown the rabbit, sprinkling as you go with salt and pepper. Remove meat from the pot and set aside. If you are making this with chicken, you might want to use less butter and olive oil, as the chicken will give off more fat.

Lower the heat, add the vegetables, and sauté for 5 minutes. Return the rabbit to the pan, add the Calvados, and let sizzle for a minute. Add the cider and the bouquet garni. Bring to a boil, lower the heat, cover, and simmer for 40 minutes, turning once at the halfway mark.

Remove the rabbit; keep warm under aluminum foil. Add honey and crème fraîche to the pan, bring sauce to a boil, reduce the heat, and simmer for 5 minutes, until the sauce thickens a bit. Return the rabbit to the pot; heat through.

Serve sprinkled with fresh chervil. Wild rice, polenta, or steamed green beans will happily share a plate.

Serves 4

GOLDEN RULES

A French kitchen is not just about what you eat, but *how* you eat. Here are my golden rules for eating *à la française*.

Eat for pleasure: Food in the United States has become something akin to fuel; you put in high-octane organic or partially hydrogenated diesel. But if your food is *only* about health or morals or social status or putting fuel in the tank, then you've got the wrong end of the baguette. Above all, French food is about pleasure, togetherness, and balance. No matter what's in your pantry, if you see food as the enemy, you'll never eat like the French.

Follow the seasons: You and your family deserve to eat good things. You deserve fruits and vegetables that taste like the best possible versions of themselves. This means cooking with the seasons. Say *au revoir* to fresh tomatoes after October; you'll meet again next summer. Get creative with mushrooms and chestnuts instead. Don't fall prey to cosmetically perfect but tasteless peaches in November; a crisp heirloom apple will do the trick. Cooking with the seasons gives rhythm to my kitchen, as my shopping evolves from winter leeks and cauliflower to spring asparagus and strawberries. Rather than thinking of nature's calendar as a constraint, I think of it like a lover's longing. Until I moved to France, I never imagined the flurry of excitement that could accompany April's first strawberries.

Shop well, cook simple: French cuisine has a reputation for being showy and complicated. But the way the French eat in their homes every day belies this—French home cooking revolves around fabulous ingredients, simply prepared. How you shop is just as important, maybe more important, than how you cook. If you stock your pantry well (legumes, whole grains, pasta, and round-the-world spices) and supplement with high-quality dairy and fresh fruits and veggies, dinner gets easier—an arts-and-crafts project rather than an episode of *MasterChef*. We often make a meal of a thick vegetable soup, cheese, and a baguette. Dessert becomes, literally, a bowl of cherries.

∽ Simple *and* Spectacular ∾

Here's a **Golden Rule recipe** that I learned from our Parisian friend Hélène, who once arrived in Céreste at 11:00 a.m. and managed to shop, cook, and have a three-course lunch on the table by 1:00 p.m. Her first course was a marvel of French improvisation—zucchini from the farm stand peeled into ribbons with a little olive oil, salt, and fresh lemon juice. A handful of toasted pine nuts gave it that perfect toothsome bite. I now use my spiralizer to make this recipe, but Hélène used a regular old vegetable peeler!

¼ cup pine nuts

4 firm medium zucchini, or 2 zucchini and 2 yellow summer squash (the mix of colors is pretty)

Juice of half a lemon

2 tablespoons olive oil

2 pinches of coarse sea salt

Freshly ground black pepper

Toast the pine nuts in a small dry frying pan.

Peel the zucchini into ribbons using only the seedless outer flesh (you can cut the part with the seeds into tomorrow morning's omelet). Combine it with the rest of the ingredients.

Serve as a first course or with whatever's on the grill.

❧ Café Conversation ❧

I pulled up a chair at the village café the other day to ask my local friends what they made for dinner on a Tuesday. *"Bien sûr,* it's five courses every night," they told me, laughing. Like the vast majority of French women, they have children and they work for a living, so on weeknights it's soup, *gratin de légumes,* a quick quiche, or croque-monsieur (the delicious French equivalent to a grilled ham and cheese sandwich, see page 171). In the summer, a big *salade composée*—what we might call a chef's salad—with sliced ham, cheese, potatoes, olives, beans, grains, and tuna. Lunch remains the more substantial hot meal; dinner is usually lighter. I found a lack of rigid separation between vegetarian and meat-based meals. Eggs, bacon, ham, or leftover chicken are often added to make a vegetable dish more substantial. A handful of cheese and a few lardons often turn what Americans might think of as a side dish into a main. A gratin can be made with Swiss chard, béchamel, and grated Gruyère, or with pasta, crème fraîche, and a can of tuna (French tuna-noodle casserole; who knew!). Relatively small portions of the main course are supplemented by bread and cheese. Oh yeah, these women are not afraid of bread—*du bon pain*—good bread, they insisted, they eat it every day.

Part Two

EQUIPMENT

I'm a low-tech cook. I don't have razor-sharp knives, a KitchenAid, or a Vitamix, and it takes me longer to retrieve, put together, and wash my food processor than it does to chop five pounds of onions by hand. I'm living proof that you don't need a cooking-show set to make delicious food. But there are a few tools in my French kitchen that I absolutely can't live without.

Secret #28

A kitchen scale: After fifteen years in France, I'm a metric convert. Baking—which is more chemistry than cooking—is easier and more consistent if you measure by weight. I put my bowl on the scale, sprinkle in the flour straight from the container, stop at 130 grams, reset to 0, then add my next ingredient, and so on. It makes cleanup quicker too—no more cups to wash. A kitchen scale makes portion control easy. I now follow the recommendations on the back of the pasta box—85 grams per person. It doesn't look like a lot, but with a heap of seasonal vegetables, it's the perfect amount in the bowl. A kitchen scale also opens up whole new continents of recipes. The rest of the world publishes their cookbooks with measurements by weight, so now I can buy that cookbook from India or Australia or Bolivia and actually use it at home!

What, Exactly, Is a Cup of Flour?

Since I moved to France, I've been cooking largely with metric measurements, where ingredients are measured by weight (grams) rather than volume (cups). A "cup" of flour can mean a lot of things. Depending on the type of flour, how you scoop, and the humidity of the flour, a cup can be anywhere from 125 grams to 160 grams! Baked goods, in particular, do not appreciate this kind of uncertainty. To get consistent measurements, you should aerate your flour with a fork before measuring (to make sure it's not packed and clumpy) and spoon the flour into the cup, rather than scooping out of the container with the cup measurement itself. Sweep a knife across the top of the cup to get an even measure. **For the recipes in this book, my cup of all-purpose flour weighs 130 grams**. Don't worry, a little more or less is not going to ruin your cake. After all, the French were cooking long before digital scales.

HAM AND ROSEMARY CHEESE PUFFS

Gougères au fromage, romarin, et jambon cru

I can think of few things I'd rather do with a cup of flour than make these. Choux pastry is one of those sexy French techniques that make you feel like a better cook—and there's very little work involved. Made with milk and topped with pebbles of sugar, choux pastry turns into my beloved breakfast *chouquettes*. Add some ice cream and chocolate sauce and you have profiteroles. Or stir in some cheese and herbs and you get these very tasty *gougères*. Crispy on the outside, moist on the inside, they are a hit at wine tastings, cocktail parties, or even a kid's birthday party.

4 eggs

1 cup finely grated Parmesan cheese

½ cup diced cured ham

⅛ cup chives, finely chopped

2 teaspoons fresh rosemary, finely chopped

Small grind of black pepper

1 cup flour

1 cup water

1 stick unsalted butter

¼ teaspoon table salt

Makes about 25 puffs

Preheat the oven to 425°F. Take the eggs out of the fridge. Combine cheese, ham, chives, rosemary, and black pepper in a small bowl and toss to distribute evenly. Measure out the flour. Have everything assembled by the stove.

In a heavy-bottomed saucepan, combine water, butter, and salt. Bring to a boil over medium heat (it is important that the mix boil—if it doesn't, your batter won't take). Turn off the heat and, working quickly, stir in the flour all at once with a wooden spoon. Immediately after, add 2 eggs and stir to combine. Immediately add the remaining 2 eggs and stir to combine; the batter should look like a lump of marzipan. Add your cheese, ham, and herbs and stir just until they are evenly distributed.

Using a lightly oiled tablespoon measure, drop rounded (not heaping) tablespoons of batter onto a cookie sheet covered with parchment paper. Leave enough room between for some puffing in the oven.

Bake at 425°F for 15 minutes. Lower the heat to 400°F and bake with the oven door slightly ajar (I stick a wooden spoon in the door), for 12 to 15 minutes more, until puffed and golden brown. Remove from the oven to a wire rack lined with paper towels (this is to remove any lingering grease from the melted cheese). Discard the paper towels and cool for a few minutes. Serve warm or at room temperature.

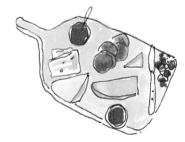

Secret #29

Le Creuset: There's a difference between something that cooks all day and someone who spends all day cooking. Many of the most beloved French dishes—beef bourguignon, seven-hour leg of lamb, the tagines of my husband's *pied noir* roots—are the result of ingredients that take a quick trip to the stove and then spend several hours in the oven. Having a heavy-bottomed pot that goes from stovetop to oven is essential. There are many brands of Dutch oven; I love my cherry-red Le Creuset. It's an investment, but it lasts a lifetime and is pretty enough to take to the table. And you don't have to do your arm exercises—lifting a full Le Creuset could be an Olympic sport.

LAMB SHANKS WITH ORANGE AND STAR ANISE

Souris d'agneau à l'orange et à la badiane

Most people have one dish in which they feel truly confident, the meal they make when new friends are coming to dinner. This is that meal for me. The combination of orange and star anise fills the kitchen with a spicy gingerbread scent; I'm almost guaranteed to get one of those "Wow, something smells good" comments as people walk in the door. If you've never tried making lamb shanks, please do—they taste great made in advance (less pre-party stress), and you'll never have to guess about quantities (a lamb shank is the very definition of an elegant single serving).

6 lamb shanks

1 to 2 tablespoons extra-virgin olive oil, plus a bit more for browning the lamb

Coarse sea salt

Freshly ground black pepper

1 medium red onion, diced

1 head garlic, cloves peeled and left whole

3 whole star anise pods

1 organic navel orange, cut into 6 sections

1 teaspoon sugar

Serves 6

1 cup best-quality tomato sauce

1 cup chicken broth

1 cup white wine

Preheat the oven to 350°F.

In a large Dutch oven, brown the lamb shanks with a bit of olive oil, seasoning generously with salt and pepper. Remove and set aside.

Add 1 to 2 tablespoons olive oil to the pot. Add onion, garlic, star anise, and orange; sauté until the mixture is lightly colored, 3 to 5 minutes.

Add the sugar and liquids; bring to a boil. Add meat back to the pot. Cover tightly and transfer to the oven. Cook for 1½ to 2 hours, until lamb is tender and sauce is slightly reduced. Let the meat rest for 15 minutes before serving, or make ahead and reheat.

Serve the shanks in shallow bowls on a bed of mashed potatoes (or Celery Root Mash, page 82). Top with the sauce, cooked orange sections, and cloves of garlic.

Secret #30

An immersion blender: The French have always made their soup the Vitamix way—minus the four-hundred-dollar gadget. French soups tend to be smooth, creamy veloutés rather than the chunky chicken noodle I grew up with. The tastes are very pure, often focusing on a single seasonal vegetable (see Creamy Broccoli Soup, page 174). The trick is to add as little broth as possible, just enough to puree. This leaves you with a thick, satisfying texture and an undiluted blast of vegetable flavor. I never add cream to my soups—the olive oil gives them a glossy richness without hiding the flavor of the vegetables.

CREAMY MUSHROOM AND CHESTNUT SOUP

Velouté de châtaignes et champignons

When the weather turns chilly and the tomatoes finally disappear from my Sunday market, I go into a kind of culinary mourning. (Until I moved to Provence, I didn't know it was possible to mourn a tomato.) I am comforted by the autumn appearance of several varieties of mushrooms. You can make this soup with white or brown mushrooms. The chestnuts add sweetness and substance, so the traditional cream you might find in a store-bought cream of mushroom soup is completely unnecessary.

3 tablespoons olive oil

1 medium onion, chopped

½ bulb fennel, chopped

1 scant cup vacuum-packed or frozen whole chestnuts

1 clove garlic, chopped

1 tablespoon cognac (optional but highly recommended)

1¼ pounds mushrooms, thinly sliced

Small pinch of salt

4 cups chicken or vegetable broth

Black pepper

Serves 4

In a stockpot, heat 2 tablespoons of the oil and sauté the onion and fennel until softened and lightly colored, about 8 minutes. Meanwhile, crumble the chestnuts into small pieces. Add the garlic, chestnut pieces, and cognac to the pot; cook for an additional 2 minutes. Transfer to a bowl and set aside.

Heat the remaining 1 tablespoon of olive oil in the stockpot. Add the mushrooms and a small pinch of salt. Cook until the mushrooms have rendered their water and most of the liquid has evaporated, 8 to 10 minutes. Remove ¼ cup of mushrooms; set aside. (This is the only soup in which Gwendal likes *morceaux*—chunks—so I save some mushrooms to chop into the finished soup.)

Add the onion mixture and the broth to the stockpot. Puree until smooth. Roughly chop the remaining ¼ cup of mushrooms; stir into the finished soup. Serve with freshly ground black pepper.

Secret #31

A crepe pan: My husband is from Brittany, the land of salted butter and sweet and savory crepes. Savory crepes—called galettes—are traditionally made with buckwheat flour, so they'll give you a hearty (and gluten-free) brunch or weeknight dinner. Make the galette your new pizza—you can top it with almost anything: ratatouille and goat cheese, smoked salmon and arugula, or, my favorite, the classic ham, cheese, and mushrooms with a fried egg on top. For the full Breton effect, make sweet crepes for dessert (see page 48).

Galettes are not hard to prepare, but a heavy-duty nonstick crepe pan is essential for success. A few rules for a happy pot: Always use heatproof plastic (rather than metal) utensils. And *never* wash your crepe pan, just wipe it clean after each use. It will gradually season—and stay nonstick forever.

TRADITIONAL BUCKWHEAT CREPES

Galettes sarrasin

4 cups buckwheat flour

1 egg

1 tablespoon melted butter or oil
  (I use olive oil)

1½ teaspoons coarse sea salt
  (or scant ¾ teaspoon fine sea salt
  or table salt)

6½ cups water

Butter, for cooking

Toppings (see facing page)

Makes about 18 galettes

Place flour in a large mixing bowl (if you have a KitchenAid or another standing mixer, this is a good time to use it). Make a well in the flour, add egg and oil, and whisk to combine. Add salt and 3 cups of water. Attach the bowl to your standing mixer and beat on medium speed for 5 to 10 minutes. I don't have a KitchenAid (though my mother did volunteer to bring hers over), so I just give it a really good, thorough whisk by hand. Gradually add the remaining 3½ cups water and whisk well to combine. Let the batter rest in the fridge for at least an hour (or, even better, a few hours or overnight). It might separate a bit, but don't worry, just whisk again when you take it out of the fridge. If it looks too thick (the desired texture is runny buttermilk), whisk in a bit more water.

Before you begin making the galettes, have your assorted toppings sliced and ready in small bowls by the stove.

Heat a 12-inch nonstick crepe pan over medium-high heat (this takes longer than you might think).

Leave some butter and 3 or 4 clean paper towels by the stove. Get out a ½-cup measure. Have your guests assembled, ready to place their orders.

When your crepe pan is nice and hot, add a small pat of butter and wipe it around with a paper towel.

The next part works best with both hands in action. Holding your scant ½ cup of batter in one hand, pick up the hot crepe pan with the other. Pour the batter in a semicircle toward the sides of the pan, then tilt the pan quickly back and forth until the batter is evenly spread in a very thin layer. (If your batter gets clumpy and sticks to one side, your pan is too hot!) Let cook for 1 minute, then run a nonstick spatula under the edges to unstick them. After that, run your spatula all the way around again, this time going about 2 inches under the galette. By now you should be able to slide your spatula under the center of the galette. Steady your nerves, and flip. Quickly add your toppings, distributing them in a thin but even layer. Cook for 30 seconds to 1 minute more. Fold your galette in half and serve. I like to fold the four edges of my galette toward the middle (you'll end up with a square shape with an area of filling peeking out in the center).

Try this

If you are feeding a crowd, you can make a stack of galettes in advance. Store at room temperature under aluminum foil; reheat directly in the crepe pan and add toppings when ready. You can use a leftover galette instead of a tortilla for a turkey wrap, or use two to make a buckwheat quesadilla.

**Secret
#32**

Madeleine molds: I normally avoid baking that requires special equipment. Madeleines are the exception. These individual scallop-shaped cakes are just too pretty, and too quintessentially French, to resist. Golden and buttery, with a hint of lemon, a madeleine is very much a live-in-the-moment treat. (They don't keep especially well, but then again, they don't need to; they'll all be gone by the next day.) I've never found anything better to accompany a cup of afternoon tea, and although I wouldn't accuse Proust of dipping, I sometimes do. Little hands love madeleines. They take no time at all to prepare; an ideal project for after-school or weekend baking. This recipe is adapted from my neighbor Catherine. We've both tried lots of recipes, and the simplest one turned out to be the best.

AFTER-SCHOOL MADELEINES

Madeleines au citron

½ cup plus 2 tablespoons sugar

Zest of 1 untreated or organic lemon

7 tablespoons butter plus ½
    tablespoon for buttering molds

1 tablespoon lavender (or other flower-
    based) honey

1 cup flour

½ teaspoon baking powder

2 large eggs

2 good pinches of vanilla powder or
    1 teaspoon high-quality vanilla
    extract

1 tablespoon fresh-squeezed lemon
    juice

*Makes 22
medium madeleines*

Preheat the oven to 400°F.

Place the sugar in a large mixing bowl and grate the lemon zest directly on top. (If you grate the lemon zest into another bowl and transfer, you lose all of those precious essential oils!) Stir to combine.

Generously butter your madeleine molds and set aside. If, like me, you are using flexible silicon molds, put them on a metal cookie sheet (you won't be able to lift the molds without spilling them once they are full).

In a small saucepan (or in the microwave), melt together the 7 tablespoons butter and the honey. Set aside to cool.

In a small bowl, combine flour and baking powder.

Add eggs and vanilla to the sugar mixture. Whisk until they are a light lemon yellow. Add butter mixture and whisk to combine. Add flour mixture and gently stir until just incorporated. Add lemon juice and stir to combine.

Fill each madeleine mold almost to the top. Bake at 400°F for 12 minutes or until golden brown. If your oven runs hot, you may have to take it down a bit. My molds are on the small side. If you have bigger molds, you may need to extend the cooking time slightly. The cakes should be nice and golden. Remove molds from the oven and cool on a wire rack for 5 minutes. Unmold the individual cakes and cool completely or serve warm. Best eaten on the day you make them; if there are any left over (unlikely), store them in an airtight container for breakfast.

**Secret
#33**

A lemon zester: This sounds like a small thing, and maybe it is, but your baking will be livelier, your sauces punchier, if you have this little tool near at hand. I always have three or four lemons hanging out in the kitchen, ready to be zested into cakes or squeezed over fish or steamed vegetables. (You should use a lemon soon after you've taken off the zest.) If I have a cold, my husband makes me hot lemon juice with honey and a shot of rum. It doesn't matter how stuffed up you are—you'll sleep through the night!

GWENDAL'S MAGIC GROG

1 heaping tablespoon honey

Juice of ½ lemon

A slug of dark rum

Serves 1

Heat the honey and lemon juice together in a nonreactive saucepan or in the microwave. Add the rum. Down. Sleeeeeep.

Part Three

RITUALS

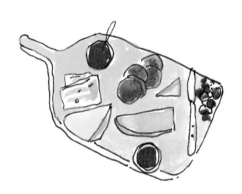

So how do they do it? How do the French eat bread and cheese, drink wine, enjoy dessert, and still look the way they do? I've spent almost every day of the past fifteen years eating at a French table, and there is no getting around this fundamental fact: The French weigh less because they eat less. Yet these people are not on a diet—this is how they *live*.

Malheureusement, you can't have the good without the bad or, rather, the strict. French society is very collective—and often very rigid. There's a time and a place for everything. It doesn't always leave space for the individual to follow his or her own path. That means that you can't decide to go buy curtains at Target at midnight and that French kids make identical art projects in preschool. Restaurants are open only at certain hours, and you will get disapproving looks if you walk down the street munching a sandwich. There are many cases where the tradition-bound, almost dogmatic aspects of French life are problematic. But where healthy eating is concerned, this cultural peer pressure is actually very helpful.

Above all, the French are very respectful of their food. French cuisine is recognized by UNESCO as a cultural treasure for the ages, just like the Pyramids and the Great Wall of China. All this glorious history means that rules and rituals are still very present in the French kitchen. A French meal is highly structured, and even the most casual meal will follow a set pattern.

Once again, I was born, and fundamentally remain, an American. I do not have the body (or the appetite) of a French pixie. I have the hips of my Russian ancestors, peasants who probably gave birth in the fields while digging potatoes. I grew up snacking indiscriminately, watching *The Breakfast Club* on the couch with a bowl of raw cookie dough. When I started working in New York and London, "lunch" was the time it took me to walk back and forth to the Korean salad bar or Pret A Manger. I don't have any more self-control than the next person. I struggle with stress-eating late at night and I have yet to permanently shed the ten pounds left over from my pregnancy. But I'm lucky enough to be living in a culture that encourages—practically mandates—healthy eating habits. And when I follow them, good things happen.

Secret #34

Sit down: "If you eat standing up, it doesn't count." That was the joke in our family, usually repeated as my mother scarfed down a 4:00 p.m. meal of leftover pork roast or muenster cheese from a Ziploc in front of the open fridge. **The French do not eat while walking, driving, or working.** Here's an example: Three weeks after my son was born, I had plans to attend my first solo post-baby event, a cocktail party and networking evening that took place on the other side of Paris. I was late, and I'd forgotten to eat lunch (as new mothers sometimes do), so at six o'clock I grabbed a *pain au chocolat* from my local boulangerie and started eating while speed-walking toward the Métro. Waiting for the light to change, I heard a voice coming from the vicinity of my knees: *"Attention aux kilos."* Was I hearing things? Maybe it was the sleep deprivation? But no. I looked down, and the homeless man sitting by the recycling bin was wagging his finger at me, telling me to watch my weight! Believe me, in France, at least where food is concerned, Big Brother really *is* watching.

Le Crouton

Thank goodness, there's an exception to every rule. The French have been known to exit the boulangerie with their baguettes (possibly still warm) and break off just the tip—*le crouton;* a two-inch piece, not a hunk. It's a little *gourmandise*—a treat for the way home. There's something perfect about the crackle and chew of these one or two bites.

Secret #35

Eat together: Dinner is where you will really get to know the French. Other than the beauty tips I've picked up from the ladies when I'm changing after yoga, almost everything I know about France I've learned *autour de la table*—around the table. I can't explain this any better than my French husband did when our three-year-old son tried to escape from the dinner table one night. "Dinner is not just about feeding yourself," Gwendal said, "it's about enjoying each other's company *en famille*—as a family." "Wait," I said, rising from the table myself to dig around for a notebook. "That's just so French, I've got to write it down." **Togetherness is the most basic tenet of French eating**—it's also the hardest for other cultures to imitate. French meals are arranged around French schedules; French employees usually have an hour for lunch, and outside of Paris, many stores are closed for several hours in the middle of the day. Family dinner remains an institution. Kids eat with their parents, usually between seven and seven thirty (many American children of my acquaintance are in bed by then). I'm realistic in my expectations. I know there's no way your average American is working just thirty-five hours a week, and it's unlikely that every family member will miraculously be home from soccer or ballet or spin class all at the same time. Still, try, even if it's only once a week.

Secret #36

Put it on a plate: The summer after I arrived in France, I threw my back out trying to drag a suitcase full of shoes up a spiral staircase. I was miserable and homesick. All I wanted to do was curl up on the couch with a container of lo mein and a DVD of *Grease*. Gwendal tried to join in my fun, but, bless his Gallic socks, he just looked so uncomfortable trying to balance an oily metal takeout container on one knee. **For the French, a meal is a civilized thing—meant to be eaten on a plate, at a table.** Plating food forces you to make a mini-occasion out of even the simplest meal. It's also essential for portion control. It's easy (at least for me) to eat a pint of mint chocolate chip out of the container, but put that same mound of ice cream in a bowl and it starts to look…unreasonable. Even—especially—if you are eating by yourself, take the time to make an attractive plate. The French would say this is a question of respect. For the food—and for yourself.

Mind Games

So much of how we eat is in our heads. Want to build in some portion control while still looking at a full plate of food? Play a little trick on yourself: Buy smaller plates. Our first summer in Provence, I spotted a set of gold-rimmed Limoges dishes at a local flea market. They were at least an inch smaller in diameter than the ones from Ikea. The same goes for wineglasses—you'll end up drinking less from a dainty cut-glass goblet than from a blown-glass whopper the size of a hot-air balloon. So go liberate your grandmother's china from the attic—you might find that in addition to offering you nice memories, it could help jump-start some healthy habits.

Secret #37

The kitchen is closed: When my mother wasn't in the mood to cook, she'd say, "The kitchen is closed." This usually meant Chinese. In France, between meals, the kitchen really *is* closed. **By and large, the French *do not snack*.** Kids have their four o'clock *goûter,* but they are not rummaging through the cabinets at all hours of the day and night. Adults don't eat between meals (unless you count tea, espresso, and/or cigarettes) or munch bags of pretzels or popcorn on the sofa after dinner. After the evening tisane and square of dark chocolate, it's lights-out. This is probably the hardest part of French eating for Americans to understand, but if you follow this rule, there are big payoffs—and not just for your waistline.

Secret #38

Enjoy being hungry: Here's a little secret. If you manage to curb your snacking, there's a reward: your food tastes better. I found that in order to cut down on my snacking, I had to radically redefine my relationship with hunger. Maybe it's Americans' collective immigrant past, but we can't stand the idea of being hungry, not for a second. It's the reflex that makes us keep protein bars in our purses, Frappuccinos in our cars, and Cheerios in the stroller. One thing I notice whenever I visit the States: I am always eating and never, ever hungry. Meals have no set time or place. By the end of a three-week visit my palate often feels like a slab of lead—all I can taste is sugar, salt, and fat. **The French know that between-meal hunger isn't deprivation, it's foreplay.** Remember your first crush, how you felt as his hand inched closer and closer at the movies? That's how I feel about dinner in France. Fifty percent of pleasure is anticipation.

✺ Bon Appétit ✺

When we visit French friends for the weekend, there's always a moment in the evening, around five thirty, when I think I'm starving to death. I eye the kids' *goûters* with envy and wonder why no one has offered me one of the leftover crepes covered with Nutella or at least an apple. Even after fifteen years in France, I still get to ask dumb questions, so I asked our friend Catherine: "But what do you do when you're hungry?" (I hope I kept the desperate whine out of my voice.) "I drink," she said. "Tea—or water." Her response lacked the urgency, the sense of instant gratification, that I as an American expect from my food. "Then I wait and see," she continued. "If I'm really hungry, I have a piece of fruit or a yogurt or a piece of chocolate. But you're supposed to be hungry for dinner," she said. "Or not hungry, exactly, but *avoir de l'appétit*—have an appetite." This got me thinking. When the French sit down to a meal, they wish one another *"Bon appétit."* Not good food, or even good health, but good appetite. Remember when your grandmother said, "Put down that cookie— you'll spoil your dinner"? This is what she meant; slight niggling hunger is a cultural prerequisite to truly enjoying what's on your plate. In France, you can't have a good meal if you don't have a good appetite.

Try this

Be a lady (or a gentleman) who lunches.

One of the ways the French avoid snacking is by eating a substantial lunch. The French still consider lunch to be the main meal of the day; if they are eating steak during the week, chances are they are doing it at noon rather than 8:00 p.m. A hot lunch is my best bet to make it through the afternoon. If I'm packing something for the office, meatballs, farro, and brussels sprouts are going to make me a lot happier than a salad.

**Secret
#39**

Hold the cheese: We recently got together with some French friends who are part of the local Rotary Club. They host foreign-exchange students every year, and all of their kids have studied in the States. "We went to visit our daughter's host family," said our friend, "and we brought them a nice *Camembert au lait cru*. They loved it, but"— and here she shook her head in bewilderment—"she served it cold from the refrigerator, *before* dinner, with some crackers and a bunch of grapes." **The French serve their cheese, often with a lightly dressed green salad, after the main course and before dessert.** Our tradition of cheese and crackers before dinner presents us with a plate of fat and carbs before we even sit down at the table—the point when we are the hungriest. Next time you have guests, keep the pre-dinner nibbles small. Instead of cheese, try olives, a small bowl of sliced cured sausage, raw vegetables, or a platter of mini-toasts spread with pâté or tapenade. A French hostess knows that hors d'oeuvres should be just enough to keep the conversation humming and that first glass of wine from going to your head.

✍ Micromanage Your Chips ✍

When I go to a casual *apéro,* a cocktail hour, in France, there will often be potato chips or unshelled peanuts present, but they will be served in something the size of a cereal bowl. No one ever takes a handful of chips (except my son, and I'm trying to cure him of that).

The Cheese Plate

Cheese is one of the great pleasures of my life in France, a part of every meal. (My father-in-law was known to eat Camembert for breakfast.) A well-chosen cheese plate is like a painter's palette, a balance of tones and textures. For a simple meal, I might offer just one kind of cheese, a mild snow-white chèvre (goat cheese) from my favorite local producer, or a fruity piece of Comté or Beaufort (always a favorite with the kids). For a more elaborate meal, three or four cheeses are the rule. I always include a variety of different strengths and types of milk. I start with one goat cheese, one cow's-milk cheese (*vache*), one sheep's-milk cheese (*brebis*), and one blue cheese, which can be made with any kind of milk. Texture is important too; I try to have at least one hard cheese and one soft oozy one. The order in which you eat the cheese has a real impact on the taste buds, so suggest that your guests start with the mild and work up to the blue (if you eat the blue cheese first, the rest of your meal might taste like ammonia).

Temp Tip: I know Americans are paranoid about refrigeration, but serving ice-cold cheese is like serving lukewarm champagne—you won't taste a thing. Let your cheese approach room temperature before serving. The flavors will really shine through.

Buy Local: French cheese may sound chic, but because of FDA rules, many of the French cheeses available in the States are the most basic pasteurized industrial brands, often with a very generic taste. When I'm in the States, I'd rather buy a washed cheese from a farm in Vermont or a sharp Wisconsin cheddar than a so-so import.

**Secret
#40**

Size matters: When I arrived in France I found the portions comically small, and I was always afraid I'd be hungry after dinner (I quickly learned that was what the cheese was for). I was surprised that even at a dinner party, there was usually only one small portion of protein per person. Why? The French weigh less because they eat less, and they eat less because they *buy* less. High-quality meat and fish are absurdly expensive. **The French will always choose quality over quantity.** I come from a Jewish American home, so I'm genetically inclined to overbuy and overcook. "If you don't have leftovers," my grandmother would say, "you didn't make enough." It's taken me years to understand that I can be a good hostess in France and not have a single spoonful left in the pot. This is not a lack of generosity—it's a question of pacing. Remember, when you finish your steak, you still have the cheese, salad, and dessert ahead. I try to think like I'm in a restaurant; you wouldn't expect to take your plate back through the swinging doors to ask for seconds if you ordered off a menu.

No doggie bags: Please, please do *not* ask for a doggie bag in France. You'll insult the chef, the waiter, the other patrons; you might even get a call from the embassy—serious diplomatic incident.

Secret #41

Fear not thy bread: A baguette is a holy thing to the French. City or country, young or old—probably the most universal French habit is buying a daily loaf of bread. Bread is present at every meal; it comes free in even the most lowly café. It is essential for mopping up sauce or cradling a slice of pâté. My mother-in-law, the essence of a teeny-tiny, weight-conscious French woman, still eats a tartine of bread and salted butter every morning with her tea, yogurt, and jam.

❧ Never Say Never ❧

Of course the French watch their weight, but they tend to make small adjustments rather than radical cuts. Instead of *no carbs* or *no sugar,* they will have a small piece of cake or limit pastry to the weekends or bread just to breakfast during bikini season. Food remains an overwhelmingly positive thing in France—it's the difference between "cheating" and "treating." The French don't think of any food as inherently bad—only excess is dangerous.

Politesse

My friend Courtney is too scared to throw her first dinner party in New York. "Having a dinner party these days is like running an obstacle course. You suddenly get this innocent little e-mail after you've planned your menu that says, "I don't eat eggs, sugar, or gluten—and I'm doing the food-combining diet so I can't mix fruit with anything else. Check out this link. See you Saturday, can't wait!" In France, unless it involved a life-or-death condition, I would never consider calling my hostess to announce what I (or my child) would or would not deign to eat. (In the case of a serious allergy, I would offer to bring my own food.) Once again, meals are among the primary building blocks of French social life, and your individual needs should not impede the pleasure of the group. That said, French meals usually include a wide variety of foods, so you can skip the bread, take an extra serving of vegetables, or avoid the cheese as needed.

Secret #42

Drink wine: I've lived in the States (where we eat without drinking) and Britain (where they drink without eating). **In France, food and drink are happily married.** I've never seen a French person (certainly not a French woman) sloppy drunk. This has to do both with what they drink (wine rather than hard alcohol) and how they drink (almost exclusively with meals). French *apéros* and dinner parties can go on till the wee hours. Learning to pace yourself means you'll never leave hungry—or stumbling.

✦

❧ Santé ❧

If you want the festive feeling of a cocktail without the sucker punch of hard alcohol, do what the French do— dress up your white wine or champagne with a dash of flavored syrup or liqueur. Cheers! Or, rather, *Santé!*

Classic: Kir Royal, crème de cassis with champagne, is a bistro classic.

Girly: For a wedding shower, add a teaspoon of rose syrup, a rose petal, and a fresh raspberry to each glass.

Festive: For the holidays, welcome your guests with glasses of champagne topped with a few fresh pomegranate seeds.

Daring: If you are lucky enough to get your hands on a fresh black truffle, grate a small pinch into the bottom of your glass, add a sugar cube, top with champagne, and stir.

Bake, don't buy: Life would be awful without cake. So bake one. I'm not suggesting you become the Cake Boss and learn how to sculpt the *Venus de Milo* out of fondant icing. Just have one or two simple recipes that your family enjoys. At the other extreme, if you really want a chocolate éclair (and who doesn't from time to time?), go and seek out a great bakery and buy yourself one—but don't buy six mediocre ones under plastic at the supermarket.

Try this

Throwing a dinner party can be a lot of work—or not. When entertaining, a French hostess often lightens the load by buying at least one course that requires no prep. Maybe it's high-quality charcuterie or olives and artichoke hearts to go with drinks. A slice of pâté with a handful of arugula or juicy melon with prosciutto makes a simple appetizer. Often, it's a beautifully crafted raspberry tart or a multilayered opera cake from her favorite patisserie. In France, it is perfectly acceptable to buy dessert for a dinner party. A French hostess knows these kinds of pastries are an art form, best left to the experts. There's no shame in not doing everything herself. On the contrary, it's a chance to support and share the work of her favorite local artisans.

PEAR SPICE BREAD

Pain d'épices aux poires

Along with the traditional yogurt cake (see page 63), this is our most frequent mother-son baking project. My son calls it "mommy cake" and I can't help but be flattered to have a dessert named in my honor, like a raspberry pavlova. Made with whole-wheat flour, olive oil, honey, and juicy pear, this is easy, guilt-free baking for any day of the week. The warm autumn spices and moist texture make it a favorite for packed lunches, teatime, or toasted for breakfast and topped with Greek yogurt and jam.

3 cups whole-wheat flour

2½ teaspoons quatre épices or pumpkin-pie spice

2 large pinches of ground nutmeg

¾ teaspoon baking powder

1 teaspoon baking soda

½ teaspoon table salt

3 eggs

1 cup olive oil

½ cup honey

½ cup brown sugar (or raw sugar)

2 cups very ripe grated pear (apples work too!)

Makes 2 loaves; each serves 6. I usually freeze the second loaf raw and bake it straight from the freezer. Start checking at 50 minutes.

2 teaspoons vanilla extract (or
    1 teaspoon of ground vanilla
    powder)

Preheat oven to 350°F.

Combine dry ingredients in a medium mixing bowl.

In a large mixing bowl, beat eggs, add oil, honey, and sugar, and whisk thoroughly to combine. Add grated pear and vanilla; combine.

Add the flour mixture to the wet ingredients in two additions; stir just enough to combine.

Grease two 9-by-5-inch loaf pans. Divide the batter between the two. Bake for about 45 minutes or until skewer comes out clean. Cool for 10 minutes. Turn out on a wire rack to cool completely. Serve warm or at room temperature.

Trust yourself

The French trust their food, and themselves around it.

They don't feel constantly in danger of going overboard. I feel

like in the States, we don't trust ourselves to stop at one cookie,

so we buy a pack of fat-free ones and eat the whole box,

searching for an elusive satisfaction that

never quite arrives.

Secret #44

You can never be too rich: The French love dessert, even if it's just a square of dark chocolate with an espresso after lunch. No proper French meal is complete without an offering of fresh fruit, plain yogurt with a dollop of jam, or the weekend treat of a *tarte au pommes* or a softhearted *fondant au chocolat*. There's plenty of butter, eggs, fruit, and high-quality chocolate, but relatively little sugar compared to American recipes. **The French like their desserts rich, rather than sweet.** But you know how the saying goes: You can never be too rich…or too thin. The key to French desserts is a skinny slice of cake, a delicate teacup of dark chocolate mousse. We're in France now; a pint of Ben and Jerry's is not a single serving.

SPICY DARK CHOCOLATE POTS

Petits pots de chocolat aux épices

This is a silky chocolate cream, so rich you'll want to serve it in espresso cups. I've infused the milk with ras el hanout, a mix of North African spices one would normally find in couscous (I think it adds just the right amount of heat and spice), but you can use orange peel, espresso, or simply a tablespoon of Armagnac instead. Add a few raspberries or a fresh fig on each saucer for an elegant finish.

1 teaspoon ras el hanout (available
   at Middle Eastern groceries
   or online)

1 cup whipping cream
   (30 percent fat)

1 cup whole milk

12 ounces best-quality dark
   chocolate, 70 percent cacao
   (I use Lindt)

2 eggs

Serves 8

Place the ras el hanout in a paper coffee filter and staple shut. In a small saucepan, combine the cream, milk, and ras el hanout. Simmer over low heat until just below boiling. (If you lose control of the milk for a minute and it boils, don't worry. Turn off the heat immediately; a skin will form while the milk rests, and you can carefully lift off the skin with a fork.) Let the warm milk infuse for about half an hour.

Finely chop the chocolate and set aside. In a small bowl, lightly mix the eggs. Ready 8 espresso cups. When the milk is finished resting, remove the coffee filter and squeeze to get every last drop of the spicy milk. Reheat the milk on the lowest possible flame until just below boiling. Add the chocolate and whisk to combine. Add the eggs and whisk quickly and thoroughly to combine. Turn off the heat and move the pot to a different burner (you want to stop the cooking process as quickly as possible). Run a spatula around the bottom of the pot to make sure everything is thoroughly combined. Carefully spoon the chocolate mixture into the espresso cups, avoiding drips. (I use a quarter-cup measure and then divide what's left.)

Tip: As with any recipe that leans on a few essential ingredients, buy the best you can afford.

ও The Frosting Diaries ও

I *love* icing—the sex, drugs, and rock 'n' roll of my adolescence was studying for my finals hopped up on a can of Pillsbury vanilla frosting mainlined with a plastic spoon. And while complaining about French pastry would be absurd in the extreme, there is a lack of icing in my new life. The first time I made my friend Betsy's famous carrot cake for my French book club, they loved the cake, but found the icing unnecessary—cloying, even. When I made my pumpkin cheesecake for Thanksgiving, I cut the sugar from a cup and a half down to one cup. It was plenty. My palate has changed a lot since I arrived in France as I adapt to the tastes of those around me. Now I understand what my friends on paleo are talking about when they say a sweet potato tastes like cotton candy.

Sweet is what we are used to.

**Secret
#45**

Liquid "off switch": I admit it—I need an off switch. A simple espresso or herbal tea at the end of the meal is a signal to the body—a long lingering taste that means dinner is over. This is particularly important for someone like me, who tends to stress eat late at night. When I'm at my parents' house in the States, we eat early and often have dessert on the couch in front of the TV—that spells disaster for me, as one ice cream pop is followed by another, and maybe some popcorn, and are there any dried apricots in the cupboard, and on and on until I've consumed far more calories than I did at dinner. If I stick to the rule that only liquid (and maybe a square of dark chocolate) passes my lips after I leave the table, I'm in much better shape (with a pleasant *appétit* for my next meal).

Doctor's Orders

The French see weight as a primary health issue. If you have a weight problem in France, you don't buy a women's magazine—you go to the doctor. I remember how embarrassed I was when my general practitioner in Provence told me I needed to lose five kilos (twelve pounds). He wouldn't let me off the hook. While he was helping me regulate my post-pregnancy thyroid issues, he was also bugging me to walk for an hour three times a week. *"Vous allez voir,"* he said, "you'll like the results and you'll start doing it more." French doctors have expectations of their patients, *hygiène de vie,* which translates literally as "life hygiene." For the French, being overweight is like not brushing your teeth—you are ignoring basic upkeep that will have profound consequences later. I have this argument with my parents all the time. I feel like they go to twelve doctors a week. The doctors shrug and, with a wry comment, give them medication, but they don't insist they make even the most basic lifestyle changes that might render some of their daily handful of pills unnecessary.

Part Four

FAMILY

The French love kids. France has the highest birthrate in continental Europe, and the very fundamentals of French life (paid parental leave, generous vacations, free universal preschool, and practically free higher education) are organized with families in mind. That said, kids in France are not running the show. French parenting is more a benevolent dictatorship than a democracy: Someone is in charge, but it's not the kids. Each child is born into an already existing family and cultural structure. Children are expected to fit into that existing lifestyle rather than remake the world in their own image. This is particularly true at the table. I'm not saying it is always easy to implement French ways in the context of American schedules, allergies, conflicting parenting methods, peer pressure, and Pop-Tarts. But if you want to do things a little differently, know you are not alone. There are entire countries—entire continents, actually—where ketchup is not a vegetable and throwing spaghetti is not a form of self-expression.

Secret #46

Never eat for two: French kids are subject to food discipline even in the womb. One reason French women stay slim throughout their lives is that they are simply not allowed to lose control of their weight during pregnancy. When I arrived for my first maternity checkup in Paris, I was given the French government handbook for expectant moms. It recommended I gain only 1 kilo (2.2 pounds) per month during pregnancy, which is about twenty to twenty-two pounds total. When I first read this, I thought it was a typo; twenty-two pounds—that's a pimple, not a pregnancy! But yes indeed, the French treat this like religion, and the midwives gently scold you if you gain more. This is not just about weight; it's about remaining the sexy confident woman you recognize, with the addition of a beautiful baby. My *sage-femme* (the literal translation of the French term for *midwife* is "wise woman") kept reminding me that a healthy fetus requires the mother to eat only an additional three hundred to four hundred calories a day—not a whole box of Ladurée *macarons*.

Secret #47

Fire the short-order cook: Stand up for your rights! You don't have to make four different things for dinner. Your kids eat what you eat. This flows from the togetherness of family meals. It's a collective time, not a time for individual complaints. The cheese and bread at the end of the meal and healthy dessert options like fruit and yogurt mean that even if your child takes only three bites of his broccoli soup, he probably won't go hungry, and you'll be reinforcing new tastes for later.

No one—I repeat, no one—is going to starve to death; I regularly see French parents denying their children food, both before and after set mealtimes. The message is this: You are a member of a society and a family. That society has rules, and as much as possible, we are going to respect them together. If you don't participate, *tant pis pour toi*. Go to your room. No one will starve to death before breakfast.

Kid Food?

Sure, there are nights when French kids eat their
classic *jambon coquillettes* (baked ham with plain
elbow macaroni), and, yes, there are sugary cereals on
the supermarket shelves. But I was surprised to find
that in France there isn't a lot that is defined as kid
food—no chicken nuggets shaped like dinosaurs or
rainbow goldfish crackers. From the very beginning,
French children eat modified versions of their parents'
meals, so if it looks weird to an adult, chances are it
won't make it to the table.

FRENCH BAKED HAM AND CHEESE SANDWICHES

Croque-monsieur

This is a meal the entire family will enjoy. A traditional croque-monsieur is made between two pieces of white bread; I like to make them open-faced—tartine-style—on whole-grain or sourdough bread.

8 slices whole-grain or sourdough bread

2½ tablespoons butter

2 tablespoons flour

1½ cups whole milk

¼ teaspoon salt

2 good pinches of nutmeg

5 teaspoons Dijon mustard

1½ cups grated Gruyère cheese

6 slices from a large baked ham

Makes 8 tartines

Preheat your oven to medium broil.

Lightly toast the bread and set aside on a cookie sheet covered with aluminum foil.

In a small heavy-bottomed saucepan, melt the butter over low heat. Whisk in the flour and stir for about 1 minute, until you get a golden color and a toasty smell. Whisk in the milk and cook over low heat, stirring pretty continuously, until the sauce is thickened, 4 to 5 minutes (it should thickly coat the back of a spoon). Turn off the heat. Stir in the salt, nutmeg, and Dijon mustard. Stir in ½ cup of the grated cheese. Leave the béchamel to cool a bit.

Top each piece of toasted bread with two layers of ham, cut to fit. Top the ham with 2 heaping tablespoons of the béchamel, followed by some of the remaining grated cheese.

Cook on the middle rack of the oven for 4 minutes, to heat through. Move up to the highest rack under the broiler for 30 seconds to 1 minute to brown. Serve immediately with a large green salad. A kid might eat one tartine; an adult might want two.

Try this

You can add a wide variety of fresh herbs to the béchamel to mix things up a bit. I make plain ones for the kids, then right at the end I add some chervil and one chopped sun-dried tomato to the remaining béchamel for a special mommy version.

Secret #48

Don't hide the veggies: Soon after I arrived in France, Jessica Seinfeld came out with a cookbook about hiding zucchini in your kids' brownies. I love zucchini bread as much as the next girl, but how did we get here? Vegetables—fresh seasonal vegetables—are yummy. The French start early, and they have lots of clever but simple tricks to get their kids to eat greens. Soup is your friend, and so are butter, olive oil, cream, grated cheese, and a sprinkle of salt. Try, as they often do at my son's school, to serve veggies as an appetizer, when kids are hungriest and willing to eat almost anything.

CREAMY BROCCOLI SOUP
(WITHOUT THE CREAM)

Soupe au brocoli

Who knew you could make dinner with nothing but an onion, a head of broccoli, and half a bouillon cube? I use the same simple method for almost all my vegetable soups. Sauté an onion, 2 shallots, or a leek in olive oil. Steam 1 to 1½ pounds of the veggie of your choice (carrot, zucchini, butternut squash, and cauliflower are family favorites) until tender. Combine all the ingredients in a stockpot with a minimal amount of broth. A quick whiz of the immersion blender and you're done.

1 large head broccoli (about 1 pound)

2 tablespoons olive oil

1 onion, chopped

Large pinch of nutmeg

Pinch of cinnamon

1 small clove garlic

2½ to 3½ cups chicken broth

Serves 4

Cut the broccoli into small florets (I also peel and chop the thick stem). In a stockpot fitted with a colander, steam the broccoli until tender but still bright green, 5 to 7 minutes. Drain the water from the stockpot; set the broccoli aside.

In the stockpot, heat the oil and sauté the onion for 5 minutes, until translucent. Add the broccoli and spices and cook together for 3 minutes. Add the garlic, stir, and cook for about 30 seconds. Then add the minimum amount of broth. Stop the heat and puree with your immersion blender until smooth. If you find the texture too thick, add a bit more broth.

Serve with bread and cheese. I've been known to top with leftover spiced chickpeas (page 18) or mix in a handful of farro (page 24).

School Lunch

In France, parents are not on their own when it comes to educating their kids about food. *La cantine,* the school cafeteria, is where even the youngest children learn the basics of healthy and varied French eating. School lunches have three courses: an appetizer, an entrée, and cheese or dessert. There is only one option for each course. In primary school, meals are served family-style; only in junior high do you get a tray and lunch line. Kids can go home for lunch, but they are not allowed to bring lunch to school, so if they stay, they eat whatever is on offer. When my son was two and a half, a new crèche (day-care center) opened in the village. Scanning the weekly menu was a revelation for me; I think his first day, it was grated carrot salad, fish with mashed potatoes, then cheese and fruit. *Aha!* I thought. *So this is how they make little French people—they start with the grated carrot salad and work up from there.* Even now, there are certain things, like creamed spinach with hard-boiled eggs, that my son will eat at school with his friends but refuses to touch at home.

◌ Tip ◌

Spiralize! I may be late to the game, but I bought my first spiralizer. Zucchini spaghetti with pesto sauce or sweet potato curly fries are great ways to get your kids to eat more fresh veggies. The prep is fun (anything with a crank handle appeals to my son) and kids are much more likely to eat something they've helped make. Here's a little recipe from the school *cantine:* Run 4 carrots through the spiralizer, toss with olive oil, salt, a squeeze of lemon juice (if your kids like lemon), and 2 tablespoons of golden raisins. Serve as an appetizer or with lettuce on a roast pork sandwich!

Secret #49

Mind your manners: Maybe this is just a personal pet peeve of mine, but on recent trips to the States, I was shocked by how seldom my son was required to use a knife and fork. Pizza, chicken fingers, sliders, spare ribs, French fries—he hardly touched a utensil. On our last trip, we sat next to a mother and her ten- or eleven-year-old daughter at the local diner. The girl asked her mom to cut her blueberry pancakes! Because French kids eat what their parents eat, they are required to use a fork and knife very early—our first French babysitter insisted my son feed himself a bowl of lentils with a spoon at the age of eleven months (messy, but true). We gave him a knife at the table when he was two and a half (he also helped me chop the zucchini for dinner—with lots of guidance, of course). The French would much rather teach table manners to toddlers (when they actually enjoy imitating adults) than to preteens (when they most decidedly do not). Eating is an important social activity; no one wants to watch *un petit cochon* (a little piggy) across the table.

∽ **Fun Fact** ∾

There's no such thing as a kid-friendly restaurant in France. They're all kid-friendly! And while you might not take your three-year-old to your Michelin-starred anniversary dinner, by and large, children are welcome (and expected to eat appropriately) at any restaurant. But don't expect a lot of kiddie amenities. Only at a fast-food joint will you find crayons or a drink served in a plastic cup with a lid and a straw. There might be a high chair or booster seat, but it's hardly a given. Some restaurants have kids' menus; many do not. In most bistros it's simple enough to order a roast chicken, pasta, or *steak haché frites* (a simple beef patty—without bread—and fries). At a recent three-course lunch at a lovely restaurant in Lourmarin, we looked up before dessert and realized there were three children (two under the age of five) sitting at the next table. We hadn't even noticed.

Secret #50

Cook together: French kids are active participants in the kitchen. My son loves to break the tips off green beans just as much as he enjoys mixing cake batter. Cooking is one of the first ways I found to really connect as a parent, and it remains one of our favorite mother-son activities. The kitchen is our dance floor, our schoolroom, our primary gathering place. Togetherness, balance, pleasure—the essence of all French meals, right from the start!

BUTTER COOKIES
WITH ORANGE-FLOWER ESSENCE
Sablés aux fleur d'oranger

When my son wants to get out his collection of cookie cutters, we make these rich sandy-textured butter cookies, flavored with just a hint of orange-flower water. Adored by kids and adults alike, they make the kitchen smell like heaven.

⅓ cup plus 1 tablespoon sugar

Zest of half an organic or
    untreated orange

1⅛ cups flour

7 tablespoons butter

2 egg yolks

½ teaspoon orange-flower water
    (available in Middle Eastern
    groceries)

*Makes 25
small cookies*

Preheat the oven to 340°F.

In a medium mixing bowl combine sugar and orange zest. Add the flour; stir to combine. Cut the butter into small cubes, add to the flour mixture, and, using two knives or your fingers, work the butter into the flour mixture until it resembles coarse crumbs. Add the egg yolks and orange-flower water and stir with a fork until the dough just comes together. Pat the dough into a flattish ball, cover with plastic wrap, and chill in the fridge for 1 hour.

Roll out the dough between two sheets of waxed paper to avoid adding more flour; it should be about ¼ inch thick. Use a cookie cutter (or the top of a small glass) to make your shapes. Bake for 15 minutes, until golden, turning the cookie sheet halfway through. Cool on a wire rack. These keep nicely in an airtight container for a few days.

Bon appétit!

INDEX

ABOUT THE AUTHOR

Elizabeth Bard is the author of the bestselling culinary memoirs *Lunch in Paris* and *Picnic in Provence.* In 2013, she and her husband created Scaramouche, an artisan ice cream company based in the small Provençal village of Céreste.

elizabethbard.com